SELL·WITH
SOUL

Creating an Extraordinary Career in Real Estate
Without Losing Your Friends,
Your Principles or Your Self-Respect

Jennifer Allan, GRI

bluegreenbooks
Denver Colorado

ISBN: 978-0-9816727-0-0

Jacket Design by Peri Poloni-Gabriel, Knockout Design
Typesetting & Design by Sheryl Evans, Evans-Studios.com
Edited by Barbara Munson, Munson Communications
First Printing May 2008
Printed in the United States of America

Published by BlueGreen Books
2932 Ross Clark Circle #452
Dothan, AL 36301
Publisher@Bluegreenbooks.com

Dedication

A huge thank you to my mother – Dorothy Allan – who has always been my biggest fan. We are so much alike... in ways we are just discovering. Thanks for reading to me every night and instilling in me not only a love of the English language, but also a deep appreciation for using it right! Love you, Mom.

acclaim for Jennifer Allan's

SELL WITH SOUL

...the writing style is engaging and the content excellent
—Jacques Werth, *High Probability Selling*

This book is absolutely amazing! I was in a continual search for finding the right book that seemed to fit me exclusively ...well, I found it!! Thank you so much, and I will definitely put the companion book to good use. I will be taking the state exam very soon, and I feel ready more than ever to pursue this dream of mine! Our personalities seem to be alike, and I always wondered how I would manage in Real Estate. But thanks to you, you've showed it can be done . . . I'm getting my home office ready now!!!
—Angela Harris, *Dallas NC*

I am reading every real estate-related book I can get my hands on, including big names like Ferry and Keller, and by far, have found your wonderful little book the most useful, helpful and entertaining. It is packed with information that is not taught in the real estate course and that is invaluable to a new agent. I can't say enough good things about your book. I admire your professionalism, your heart and ethical conduct; you are the agent I aspire to be once I am in the business.
—Jamie Carlson, *SK Canada*

I love your book so far! Very entertaining and encouraging for a brand new agent! I hope to become more like you.
—Tarayn Comer, *Birmingham, Alabama*

It should be required reading for every real estate agent. Jennifer shares her rise from a nervous rookie agent to a successful real estate broker in this warm, witty and relatable guide. This book is an answer to every new agent's daily quandary: What do I need to do today to succeed and how do I do it?
—Nicole Lincoln, *Houston TX*

I absolutely LOVE the book! I'm half-way through, taking notes with just about everything, and have learned so much ... I apologize for going on and on, but I'm just so darn excited with your book! Thanks for your wonderful insight to the whole real estate profession!"
—Mary Whitaker, *Clyde OH*

Sell with Soul has all the excitement of a good novel, yet it delivers tons of solid information. Author Jennifer Allan loves to write and it shows. It is a refreshing change from cookie-cutter business and how-to books that forget to put the reader into the equation. If I were a new real estate agent, this book would be at the top of my list.
—Barbara Munson, *Golden CO*

Great information! The advice you give regarding buyers and investors is very informational! A new agent will not have gone through these experiences and if they find themselves with Priscilla or with an out-of-town client this chapter will give them a heads up on how to handle them. To be able to determine whether they should go on—or help them understand that sick feeling in their stomach when thinking about taking Husband out for the thousandth time while Wifee is working.
—Elizabeth Nelson, *Gresham OR*

For anyone who works their sphere — or wants to do so successfully -- you MUST read Jennifer's book, Sell With Soul. I just finished reading it and cannot say enough good things about it. She describes to a "t" how I run my business and I feel I have been pretty successful without a whole lot of sweat equity, so I can say with 100% certainty what she has to say WORKS. And works well.
—Susan Haughton, *Alexandria VA*

After selling real estate for thirty years, I've read and listened to every trainer in the business! I always wondered when someone was going to focus on both integrity and making money. Jennifer has done just that with style, humor and insight.
—Michael Robinson, *Long Beach, California*

Just checking in to say I LOVED your book! It felt soooo good to hear from someone who has been successful validate my belief system as it relates to this business. I passed it on to a friend, who also "sells with soul!" and she had high praise for it. I think there are a lot of soulful agents out there who need to understand they do not have to be follow Buffini or Ferry or Proctor or anyone else whose words just do not resonate with them and whose style just doesn't work for them.
—Susan Haughton, *Alexandria VA*

This book is an excellent resource for a new real estate agent, or even a more seasoned agent who is tired of sending out farming postcards to 2000 strangers every month. Instead of spending tons of money on stuff that the vast majority of your recipients will simply throw away, Jennifer encourages you to use your valuable resources and time by fishing in the "friendly pond" by building on relationships you already have.

A lot of what you will read is good common sense; not necessarily "revolutionary" but will leave you smacking your head, saying 'Now, why didn't I think of that!?'
—Karen, *Amazon.com review*

I love your book! I'm reading it every chance I get and am almost finished. Thanks so much for writing it. Selling with Soul is the only way to sell in my opinion and you gave it a name!
—Vickie Teel, *Tennessee*

I read Sell with Soul last night and ended up dog-earing most of the pages. I laughed, I cried... at one point, I started to wonder if you had been stalking me during my first year! I wish I'd had the book then. You're an excellent writer and your book gave me some creative ideas and solutions to problems I still face – thank you!
—Robin Rogers, *San Antonio, Texas*

Your book has become my bible. I have bought so many manuals and all of them give way too much information and are confusing. Your book is so easy to understand and has great information. Reading it was like you were having a conversation with me. I've actually read it twice!
—Francesca Novak, *Lake Oswego, Oregon*

I wanted to read your book because I've always admired the way you handled your business. Like you, I don't do any of the 'Old School' things I'd be way too embarrassed. I think $14 bucks is a ridiculously cheap price to pay for your advice!
—Betty Luce, *Denver CO*

I am only half way through the book and so far you've hit every nail on the head. Great work! You are the real deal. Both new and seasoned agents should read this.
—Loreena Yeo, *Frisco TX*

You are my hero! I loved your book. It was extremely well-written: conversational and informative without being preachy or condescending. Your message is like a session with a patient mentor.
—Michelle Somers, *New York*

Acknowledgements

In the first edition of Sell with Soul, I forgot to acknowl-edge the Very Important People who helped me along the way to my first published book. Shame on me.

First, I want to thank Barbara Munson my editor (www.munsoncommu-nications.com), without whom the first edition of Sell with Soul would have faded into oblivion among the thousands of other newly released books in 2007. Barbara gently led me to the concept of SOUL and somehow managed to overcome my stubbornness and ego-maniacal tendencies to convince me that she knew what she was doing. Now that, my friend, takes tact! And of course, lots and lots of talent. Thank you, Barb.

To my family who eagerly helped me proof-read and fine-tune Sell with Soul, even though none of them cares much about real estate. I come from a family of grammar-philes, so the input was invaluable. Julie – you've always been my biggest fan (after Mom, of course); Janice – you are such an inspi-ration to me, so your praise really meant a lot; Tom & Lynn – I loved that you both loved the book and were so forthcoming with your compliments; THANK YOU.

And of course, my mother, to whom this book is dedicated and is the most influential person of my 41 years on the planet.

Ken Edwards – You crack me up! I'm so glad we met – your input and advice has been an enormous help to me and I'll always remember you as my "first" – as in my first published review!

Crystal Pina (www.VisionsVirtualAssistance.com) – Thanks for pushing me out of my comfort zone in early 2007. I fought you tooth & nail (what does that mean anyway?) but you prevailed. Thanks so much for all your help and all the great ideas that came from our brainstorming sessions.

Cari Frank – I'll bet you're surprised to see your name here Cari! Even though we haven't talked for ages, YOU were the original inspiration for Sell with Soul. Years ago, Cari mentioned to me that the real estate training she received at her Big Name company wasn't helping her a bit and she wished someone like me would create a training program that actually teaches new agents HOW to sell real estate. Wow – what a concept!

Julie Cooper – Meeting Julie changed my life in many ways. Julie was my business partner and friend during the later years of my real estate career. She made it possible for me to try things that I previously considered impossible, and many of the lessons I share in SWS are a direct result of my relationship with Julie.

Dave Pike (www.ThePikeGroup.com) – My very first real estate mentor in 1996. So much of what made my career successful came directly from my friendship with Dave. He graciously took me under his wing – without pay I might add – and taught me the finer points of a competency-based real estate philosophy. Again, much of what you will read in SWS is directly related to the fact that I met Dave Pike those many years ago.

Thanks to the founders of Active Rain (www.activerain.com) who created an amazing vehicle for me to get my Soulful message out to thousands of real estate agents across the country and around the world. I hope you guys get filthy, stinking rich from your creation because you've certainly enriched the lives of so many of us.

To all my loyal readers – you guys rock. I started to make a list here of everyone else who has made this journey so special, but the list went on and on...and I was petrified of leaving someone out. You know who you are and I hope you know how much I appreciate your feedback, comments and support. The SWS message attracts the smartest, coolest, most creative agents in the world!

table of contents

welcome to sell with soul...

Y ou have a choice to make. Today. And tomorrow. In fact, you will make a very important decision every day you work as a real estate agent, from today until the day you retire from the business.

Each and every day, you'll have to choose between Right and Wrong. Fair or Unfair. Respectful or Disrespectful. Every time you meet with or talk to a client...a prospect...a buyer...a seller...every time you make a judgment call or "executive decision" on a matter with no clear-cut answer...you'll need to choose on which side to hang your hat. The side with Soul...or No Soul.

What are some dilemmas you might face? Here are a few to ponder...will you pursue a referral fee from your brother's real estate agent? Should you encourage a bidding war on your brand new listing? Will you refuse to show your listing to a buyer who already has a buyer agent? Should you take advantage of the opportunity to learn an unfamiliar market with a new buyer? How much will you charge your first seller client? We'll discuss all these situations and many more—and you may be surprised by the "soulful" choices I recommend.

I'd like to tell you that if you make too many un-soulful choices you will fail miserably in your real estate career. I'd like to tell you that, but I'd be lying (and that would be un-soulful!). Unfortunately, thousands of real estate agents have experienced wild financial success treating their clients and associates disrespectfully and, well, like dirt.

This has not gone unnoticed by the general public; real estate salespeople "enjoy" a Top Five ranking in a recent list of the nation's most un-trusted professions. Ouch! We're up there with car salesmen and politicians, a fact largely due (in my humble opinion) to what I call the "Old School" of real estate thought and training.

You may already be familiar with the Old School philosophies. According to the Old School, the way to succeed selling real estate is to treat it like a numbers game. To use condescending sales scripts, hard-core prospecting techniques and high pressure closing strategies. Old School agents are frequently depicted in the movies as greedy, self serving creeps. Unfortunately, these characters weren't invented by screen writers; they are alive and well and working in your neighborhood. And some are even making a pretty good living.

But I'm guessing that if you purchased a book called "Sell with Soul," you're hoping there is a better way. A way to succeed without sacrificing your soul to do so. While you may freely admit that you want to make lots of money (and there's nothing wrong with that!), you'd prefer not to make it at the expense of your integrity or dignity.

Or, let's be blunt here, maybe you don't consider yourself particularly soulful, but you doubt your ability to use the methods you've been taught by Old School trainers because they're just too "salesy" for you. You cringe when you imagine yourself making 100 cold calls a day, or putting those tired old closing techniques into play. You might even feel inadequate that you aren't overly enthusiastic about pestering strangers for business.

Quite simply, you know in your heart (and soul) that something is wrong with the advice of the Old School masters, yet you worry that you might not be successful unless you follow it.

Well, take heart—I have terrific news for you! You absolutely, positively can succeed in real estate sales without resorting to Old School methodology! And when I say succeed, yes, I mean you can make a ton of money, but oh, so much more.

A successful career selling real estate can be a beautiful thing. An extraordinary thing. If you are a great real estate agent, that's something to be proud of. And chances are, if you are great, you will love your job. Can you imagine bouncing out of bed in the morning, every morning, eager to get to work? Or not dreading the end of your vacation because you're so excited about getting back to your business? Itching to check your voicemail messages because you can't wait to find out who called you while you were in the dentist's chair? If you've never experienced the euphoria of doing a job you love, and being well-paid to do it, ahhhh, you have something wonderful to look forward to.

With that, I welcome you to Sell with Soul. The Sell with Soul approach is radically different from the vast majority of real estate sales training programs out there. Selling with Soul centers around r-e-s-p-e-c-t. Respecting our clients — buyers, sellers, customers, prospects. Treating them like intelligent, competent human beings who don't need a lot of slick sales B.S. to make the right decision. Who don't need to be smoothly "closed" in order to sign the paperwork that secures our all important paycheck.

To Sell with Soul means that we acknowledge and appreciate the generous "contributions" our clients make to our children's college educations (in the form of real estate commissions). That we are willing to part with a few of our precious commission dollars when it's the right thing to do. Especially when we screw up. But even when we don't. That we care as much about the clients we have now as the clients we hope to have in the future. When our FOR SALE sign goes into a yard, we truly care about selling that home as much as our client does.

It means that when we forget to put our client first (it will happen), we at least feel bad about it. We might even <gasp> 'fess up and apologize.

When you Sell with Soul, you learn your job at your own expense, not at the expense of your paying customers, your buyers and sellers. You are competent. You know your market, your systems and your contracts. You are a good negotiator.

Not one of the tips, techniques, opinions or strategies found in this book is insulting or patronizing to your client. All my suggestions have clients placed firmly in first position, where they belong, and where your agency agreements (legal documents, remember) declare them to be. You'll find none of the hostility or cynicism toward your clients here that you may encounter elsewhere. Even in (especially in) your own real estate office.

I HAVE A CONFESSION...

I'm not a people-person. I'm not shy, exactly, just...socially uncomfortable. Small talk is a foreign language to me. If I spend a day showing buyers around town or even holding a three-hour open house, I'll need some time alone to recharge afterwards. Cold calling or door knocking to prospect for business? You're kidding, right? You won't find me at any chamber of commerce networking event; heck, I get anxious about going to closings!

Not the best profile for a successful real estate agent, huh?

But I am successful! And not because I am pushy, schmoozy or even particularly friendly. Just the opposite, in fact. Can I sell snow to Eskimos? Nope. Can I sell 75 homes a year? Yep. No problem.

I succeed in real estate sales, not because I'm charismatic, but because I am Very Good at my Job. Good at the details, good at negotiating, good at the follow up. And no one is better than I am at creatively solving problems. Since I can't dazzle them with my charm, I have to blow them away with my competence.

I went into real estate sales on a whim, like so many others. My big plan was to get my license and make my fortune buying hot investment properties...and maybe sell a few homes along the way (sound familiar?). I knew I'd never be successful if I had to knock on doors or dial-for-dollars, which is the "only" way to succeed, right? Well, that sure wasn't going to happen, so I figured I'd just hope that enough friends would hire me so I could pay the bills while I built my personal real estate empire.

But it didn't happen that way. Somewhere along the line I fell in love with my new career. I actually enjoyed selling real estate! No one was as surprised as I was when the sales results were tallied at the end of my first year, and I was the second highest producing rookie out of 75 new agents. Okay, so I didn't set the world on fire, but I was doing something right. And believe me, it didn't involve calling up strangers or pestering By-Owner sellers.

This is not to say I didn't consider the traditional sales methods. Sure, I purchased and read all the guru books recommended to me...I say I read them... but I can't say I followed much of the advice I found within those sacred texts. Many of the techniques for cold calling, door knocking and farming left me cold and I sincerely doubted my ability to stick with programs that admittedly involved, even celebrated, cold hard rejection.

For those of you who shudder at the thought of chasing down your prey, this book is for you. First, I'll help you build your business using respectful, non-invasive techniques. No farming, cold calling or door knocking. You won't have to hunt down For Sale by Owners (FSBO's) or Expired listings if you don't want to.

But more importantly, I'll help you to quickly develop the knowledge, skills and attitude to truly be an extraordinary real estate agent. An agent who, even during her rookie year, will inspire her friends to excitedly refer her to their friends and associates. When you're really, really good at your job, and you know it, you exude confidence. My friends and clients laugh at me when I tell them I'm socially inept...more than once I've been told I'm one of the most confident people they know.

My professional confidence comes from knowing I'm a good real estate agent. Now put me in a room full of people who aren't interested in my real estate expertise and you'll find me hiding in the corner, slinking toward the exit as quickly and unobtrusively as possible. So, no, unfortunately, my professional confidence has never translated into social confidence. Ah well.

But I digress. Sell with Soul was written to help you build an extraordinary business using techniques and strategies that are far more respectful to your prospects and clients than the Old School methods. To help you develop the skills and expertise that will enable you to enthusiastically promote yourself and your services to the home-buying and -selling world out there.

SO WHO AM I...

...to give you advice on building a successful real estate business? Well, I'm not Tom Hopkins or Mike Ferry or Brian Buffini (names you have probably heard—if you haven't, you will). I never made a million dollars a year selling real estate and I never had ten buyer agents working under me. I was not the top producing agent in my city, nor did I ever qualify for any national lists of the most successful agents.

But I did well. Quite well. As mentioned, my first year I was runner-up for Rookie of the Year and was later the perennial top agent in my office. My first full year in the business I earned around $70,000; my best year was $332,000. When I stopped selling real estate full-time, I could easily count on bringing in at least $200,000 by working four to six hours a day. Sound good?

My real estate career started off in the traditional fashion...go to school, pass the test, find a brokerage firm to hire me. But because I've always been a bit of a loner, by my second week I found myself working from home most of the time. By working from my home office, I missed out on the inevitable training-by-osmosis that occurs when you hang out in a busy real estate office... eavesdropping on the prospecting and closing techniques of other agents, watching the administrative staff process listings and closings, participating in the daily (hourly?) gripe sessions. I didn't get to listen in as the Top Dogs refused to negotiate their listing commissions, I didn't learn (from others) how to resolve a tough inspection. But neither did I waste all day Wednesday (tour day) with a bunch of other agents who would never refer business to me.

I rarely saw my broker, so I was forced to solve my own problems, my own way. In other words, I developed my real estate expertise without a lot of distracting input from others. I might have recreated the wheel a few times, but overall, I feel that I created a better wheel and ran my business in a more professional, more creative and more client-centered fashion than many of the other agents I have run into.

About seven years into my career, after working from home all that time, I got the wild idea that I should immerse myself in the real estate culture and Go To The Office Every Day. Wow, oh wow—my first experience in the real world of real estate. Sitting at my crummy desk, listening to the other agents use contrived sales scripts that were utterly condescending to anyone with intelligence, hearing the tired old listing and commission negotiating strategies ("No, I won't reduce my commission. If I can't hold firm negotiating for myself, how effective do you think I'd be negotiating for you?"). The farming campaigns that (to me) were tacky and unprofessional. They worked, I guess, but it was hard for me to imagine putting my name on that garbage.

My experiment lasted about six months before I couldn't take it anymore. Although the other agents were a constant source of entertainment, I hadn't realized how mired in Old School tradition most of the real estate world still is. I was dismayed at the continuing blatant disrespect many real estate practitioners have for their clients and fellow salespeople. And the greed—oh my. But I'll talk more about that later.

WHY SELL WITH SOUL?

Lest you believe that I advocate the Sell with Soul approach only because I want to improve the reputation and public perception of the real estate industry, let me make one thing crystal clear. Selling with Soul will make you money. It might even make you rich. But not due to any universal cosmic karma. Not even because buyers and sellers will flock to your door 'cause you're so cool. Sure, that will happen, especially as your referral business gains momentum, but, no, a big reason you'll make more money isn't just because you'll have more business. It's also because, by being soulful (i.e., competent, attentive and respectful), the real estate deals you work so hard to put together will close. Not only will you be able to recognize and solve the deal-breaking problems that threaten your paycheck every day, but as a soulful agent, you can keep everyone calm during chaos. People buying and selling homes get emotional, even irrationally so sometimes, and an out-of-control, ego-driven Old School agent often makes things worse.

Throughout this book, you will see many specific examples of Selling with Soul. You will see how a soulful real estate agent wields tremendous power over his or her business by simply being competent and following the Golden Rule. And that power is intoxicating.

If you believe, as I do, that a real estate transaction can be a win/win for everyone, and that at the end of the day everyone can still be friends, you have SOUL!

Be yourself. You don't have to be some hyped-up, blue-suited, smiley-faced "sales professional" to enjoy extraordinary success in real estate. You don't have to memorize scripts, make 100 cold calls or knock on strangers' doors. Unless you want to. Truly, you can wake up every morning, put on your own face and set the world on fire selling real estate. And enjoy every minute of it. Okay, most minutes.

PLEASE NOTE...

The majority of my real estate experience, both personal and professional, has been in Colorado. Therefore, some of the terms I use may be unfamiliar to you if you work in a state with significantly different laws and practices. For example, Colorado is a table funding state, which means that money exchanges hands at the closing table even though the documents have not yet been recorded. Sellers get their proceeds, real estate agents get paid, buyers get the keys. Some states, like California, are escrow states, which means there is no actual "closing" ceremony and funds are disbursed after all documents are recorded. When I use the term "under contract," it means essentially the same thing as "in escrow." I have tried to make my suggestions and instructions general enough to help you through the various processes despite minor or even major differences among markets. If something you find in this book sounds way off base, please check with your broker for clarification before putting my words into action!

Most of the names and events depicted throughout this book have been altered to protect the innocent and the not-so-innocent. Many anecdotes come from my own personal experience, but others have been gathered over the years from my friends and colleagues.

Jennifer Allan

OF SPECIAL INTEREST
TO THE "SOCIALLY UNCOMFORTABLE"

Celebrating the Introvert Within

The original title of this book was Real Estate for the Shy, An Introvert's Guide to a Wildly Successful Career in Real Estate. I wrote 75% of Sell with Soul with the intent of lighting a fire under all the introverted real estate gods and goddesses out there who didn't realize they could compete successfully in a career dominated by charismatic "natural" salesmen and women.

I was really excited about my book for introverted real estate agents. Never mind

> WHAT'S THE DIFFERENCE BETWEEN AN EXTROVERT AND AN INTROVERT?
>
> *An extrovert is someone who gets his or her energy from being around others; an introvert is someone who is energized by being alone. When an extrovert is left alone for long periods of time, he becomes lethargic. Conversely, an introvert will be exhausted and drained after a day of social interaction.*

that most real estate agents aren't introverts. Never mind, in fact, that the majority (75%) of the general public consider themselves to be extroverts. I was too committed to my concept to give up easily, even under pressure from numerous naysayers who were convinced I was nuts to put my heart (and soul) into a book written for a virtually non-existent population.

Thank God for my editor, Barbara Munson. Being an introvert herself, she supported my concept and appreciated what I was trying to accomplish. But one day, she made a casual observation that changed not only the direction of this book, but also the direction of my writing career. She said "I don't really think that you were successful because you were an introvert, it seems that you were successful because you had soul." After much discussion as to what "soul" actually meant, I decided that yes...that must be it, I am soulful! And, of course, humble.

However, interestingly enough, the most vigorous praise I've received for Sell with Soul comes from...you guessed it...introverted agents! Because I have freely admitted that I'm not a social butterfly, many agents have written to me confiding they, too, are a little shy around strangers and have secret concerns about their longevity in the business. I have developed many online friendships with introverted agents across the country and even around the world, and am thoroughly enjoying watching them flourish and prosper using strategies they learn from me.

Because Sell with Soul was written by a fellow introvert, the ideas and recommendations presented will feel natural to you. You are probably already a bit of a stickler for details. You are probably already reliable, organized and efficient. These skills will take you much further than you might suspect in your real estate career.

And you know what? Your natural personality may very well be a big factor in your success. If you consider traditional real estate prospecting and closing techniques too invasive and assumptive for your personality, you will develop your own style that, as a by-product, shows respect for your prospects and clients. You will treat them as intelligent human beings, which they will truly appreciate and find refreshing.

So, embrace your natural personality—it's not something to be overcome; it's something to celebrate!

what you didn't learn in real estate school
...the realities of a career in real estate

So—Are You Ready to Sell with Soul?

Welcome to the Wonderful World of Real Estate Sales! If you're fresh out of real estate school, you are about to begin a career that can lead you to fame and fortune...or sadly be an unfortunate blip on the radar screen of your professional life. Statistics quote figures that range from 70% to 95% dropout rate for first-year real estate agents and it's common knowledge in the industry that only a small percentage of the licensed agents are making enough money to live on...selling real estate, that is.

If you get through your first year with your enthusiasm intact, you will have beaten the odds and stand an excellent chance of success. And success selling real estate is a beautiful thing. A career in real estate sales offers nearly unlimited potential for financial reward, an enviable lifestyle, and the opportunity to build an empire for your retirement or to pass on to your children. It can also guarantee you a captive audience at social gatherings, if that's your thing.

Why is the failure rate so high? It's not as if real estate is brain surgery; there are thousands of non-rocket-scientist real estate agents out there making plenty of money. It's not a matter of supply and demand; there's plenty of business to go around, even in a slow market. Is it a matter of unrealistic expectations?

Maybe. A lack of enthusiasm? Probably. A lack of support and training? Absolutely.

Funny, they don't teach you how to sell real estate in real estate school. They teach you how to pass the state exam. If you passed the test, your real estate school did its job. Moreover, the training provided by Big Name real estate companies is geared primarily toward teaching new agents to prospect, with little guidance on how to actually be a competent real estate agent.

But you may not be worried about that just yet, especially if you're new.

Brand new real estate agents have an arrogance about them (we all did)— especially if we bought or sold a few homes of our own in our past life. We think we know it all and are ready to take the real estate world by storm. Get out of the way, hot shot agent coming through! Then reality creeps in. Our ignorance starts to show.

Maybe it happens when you're scheduling showings for your first buyer. Or when you're sitting down to write your first offer. Perhaps, like me, you panicked when you got your first listing under contract and had no idea what to do then. Or, also like me, when you stayed up 48 hours straight trying to put together your first market analysis. Most likely, all these scenarios will happen to you and provide periodic reality checks to keep you humble.

Or, perhaps, drive you screaming (or whimpering) from the business.

As a professional real estate agent, you will be well paid for your services, and your clients expect you to be competent at your job, not just competent at prospecting. Your paying clients don't care if you have ten listings or two, if you have five upcoming closings or none. They do care deeply that you understand the real estate market, that you're a good negotiator and that you know how to look after them and their needs.

Most new agents learn the nuts and bolts of their business the hard way. Often at the expense of their paying clients and, consequently, at the expense of their own checkbook (if they're honorable). I'm going to try to help you avoid some of the costly or embarrassing mistakes, but believe me, you'll suffer your share of them anyway. Try to grin and bear it—it's true that you learn more from your mistakes than from your successes.

After six months or so in the business, you will have (hopefully) muddled your way through most of your "first times" and are feeling cocky again. Enjoy it—it won't last. The degree of difficulty of the challenges you encounter throughout your real estate career will increase in direct proportion to your experience and competency, always pushing you beyond your comfort zone. Just when you're feeling in control again, BAM! You'll be blindsided by an obscure FHA regulation or threatened with a lawsuit over a "non conforming" bedroom.

Real estate transactions have many players, all of whom have their own (ever changing) rules of engagement. Most of these players are not interested in helping you learn their rules unless you show great promise and potential to make them money.

THE MYTHS AND REALITIES OF A CAREER IN REAL ESTATE

When I think back to real estate school, it seems to me I remember a bunch of cocky, arrogant, middle-aged folks who were ready to set the world on fire. Real estate school was just a formality—they already knew it all. They smoked their cigarettes at break and regaled each other with grand stories of future riches and grandeur. Most of them claimed to already be "set up"—they were being sponsored by some hot shot broker or builder, or were going to be part of a fix-n-flip investment team and make a million in a few months. I don't think any of us thought we'd take the traditional route of building a real estate business from scratch.

Had you asked these students why they thought they would succeed selling real estate, you'd have gotten a variety of answers. Since statistically it's likely most of them didn't succeed, we probably shouldn't give their opinions a lot of weight; indeed, most new agents have no idea what it takes to be successful, nor what to expect from a real estate career.

The general public's view of real estate agents is that we sit at open houses on Sunday and drive people around on Saturday. During the week, we look at more houses, just for fun. That's about it. When I decided to go to real estate school, all I knew about the job was what I had seen my real estate agent do and figured, heck, I could do that. Probably even better. That's what we all say.

Why do you think you'll be successful selling real estate? Because you Love People and Love Houses? If you are successful, it won't be because you love people and houses. As the skeptics say... "Sometimes love is not enough." I never have particularly loved strangers and I was sick of looking at houses after about a year in the business. But I still enjoyed my job and I was definitely in that percentage of successful agents making a good living.

So, let's take a look at some of the myths you might be carrying around with you about the business of real estate and see if we can't shake things up a little bit for you.

■ Myth #1

Your Love of People
Will Make You a Successful Real Estate Agent

"She's not the friendliest person in the world, but she gets the job done" is how one of my biggest clients described me to a referral. After I picked myself up off the floor, I decided she meant it as a compliment, since obviously, she seemed satisfied with my service. And who am I kidding? No one has ever accused me of being a natural salesperson.

A general liking and appreciation for other people is a dandy characteristic for anyone to have, especially someone who has chosen sales as a career. But real estate isn't sales in the traditional sense. The only product you're selling is yourself; the rest of your job is primarily service related. If you are a people-person, great. It will help you be a successful real estate agent and possibly happier and more fulfilled overall. But if you're like me, with a natural tendency to shy away from social situations, don't fret. You can still be wildly successful in real estate.

But if, like me, you won't be able to distract them with your charm, you'll need to blow them away with your expertise. And responsiveness. And confidence.

I once had a partner who was more of the warm fuzzy type. Whenever we tag-teamed a client (i.e., we both showed them homes or shared the listing), we always laughed at how she knew all the details of their personal lives and I didn't even know the ages of their children or what exactly the clients did for a living. I'm all business and don't mess around with small talk.

Not surprisingly, some clients loved her and disliked me, yet others preferred my efficiency and expediency. Different strokes. If you are the friendly type, you will attract and please a certain type of client. But if you're more like me—don't worry, there are plenty of "just-the-facts" real estate buyers and sellers out there who will think you're great. As long as you are good. I'm here to help you with that.

■ *Myth #2*

Your Love of Houses
Will Make You a Successful Real Estate Agent

This is probably the number one reason people choose real estate as a career. They loved the house-shopping process when they bought their first home and thought, "Gee, I could do this all day, this is fun!" And it is, at first. But after a year or two, the thrill is gone. You will know, from looking at a house from the street, pretty much what to expect on the inside. "Ah, a 1928 brick bungalow—narrow living room and dining room on the left, two bedrooms and a bath on the right, small kitchen in the back, stairs leading to the basement off the kitchen."

You'll get tired of struggling with jammed or frozen lockboxes. Your knees will scream in protest as you explore yet another two-story home with a finished basement. You'll despair as you realize that the owner of the home you're showing is home and intends to show you and your buyer every single closet personally.

I had a Ph.D. client (a special breed) who insisted on photographing every room of every house we looked at. Yes, even homes he had absolutely no interest in. Then he would take notes in his spiral notebook so he wouldn't forget what he'd taken pictures of. With approximate room measurements. Looking at eight homes with this guy would take far longer than the two hours I allowed.

While liking homes won't make you a success, having a working knowledge of home construction, your local architecture and a general idea of the cost of repairs just might. Your job as a real estate agent is not to Ooh and Aah over homes with your buyers, but to advise them on the issues that are important to them. Such as the cost to replace a 50-year-old furnace (the electrical may need to be upgraded and the chimney lined). Or that this particular lakefront neighborhood has a high water table, so we need to check out the sump pump.

Or what to advise your buyer when a home smells like cat urine or cigarette smoke.

Maybe you'll never reach the point of buyer burnout, and if you don't, good for you. But don't go into real estate because you think you'll always enjoy a good day of house-shopping with your clients.

- *Myth #3*

You Have to Pester (er, Cold Call)
Strangers to Build a Successful Business

Some people have it, some don't. The desire and willingness to cold call, door knock and network, that is. I'll bet many competent future real estate agents have been deterred from their calling, thinking that they had to spend their lives bothering people to get their business. Not true! I am living proof of that and so are countless other successful real estate agents.

Strangers are probably not your best source of business anyway. Many real estate agents primarily prospect to strangers with newspaper advertising, web placement, bus bench ads, even billboards, but these self-promotion techniques are expensive. I've found that the agents who attribute their success to these techniques are the ones who could not pay the bills relying on a referral-based model. In other words, they don't get many referrals! Possibly because they are spending most of their time and energy on massive marketing projects rather than focusing on doing a good job for the clients they already have.

I've known many agents who operate this way. Their marketing efforts are legendary. They blanket their farm area with thousands of postcards, harass every expired listing, advertise on the radio and TV and pay big bucks for top placement on search engines. And they do get a lot of business, so I guess you could say these efforts are successful. But that's not the way I'd want to build my business.

(If the above sounds good to you, see if you can get a refund for this book. It won't be much use to you.)

It doesn't have to be that way. You can build a successful business on a combination of referrals and warm prospecting, which we'll discuss in depth later. Just know that if the thought of making a hundred phone calls a day asking the poor sap who answers the phone if he "knows anyone who's thinking of buying or selling real estate?" leaves you cold, don't for a minute think that you can't be as successful as you want to be.

▪ Myth #4

Your Job Is to Drive Buyers
Around and Hold Open Houses

Because these are the most visible activities of a real estate agent, you may believe that this is pretty much what you do. Be grateful it's not! You'd die of boredom in six months. No, real estate is much more about problem solving, follow-up and customer service. These are the areas that will make or break your career.

▪ Myth #5

You Will Work Every Weekend

Surprise! You probably won't. Again, since you (and the general public) may think that your primary activities are open houses and showing houses to buyers, it's reasonable to expect that you'll work all weekend and rest on Monday. Not true. If you have a buyer or two, you may show them homes for a few hours on Saturday, but not as often as you think. If you do open houses (and you probably should), you may take up much of your Sunday preparing for and holding the open house.

But a major function of your job is to solve your clients' problems. The people who are going to help you do this work M-F 9:00 to 5:00. That's when you'll clock most of your hours. In your first few years, you may not have as much structured time off as you're used to, but you will certainly have plenty of time to do your laundry, your grocery shopping and even your workout. You just fit it in around the schedules of your clients. Real estate offers the Illusion of Controlling Your Time!

I hardly ever worked weekends. Why? Because Coloradans like to play in the mountains on their days off. They don't want to waste their Saturdays looking at homes, and if it's a good powder day at Vail, the phone doesn't ring at all.

- *Myth #6*

Real Estate Is a Team Sport

Real estate is an individual sport. Period. No one in your office or corporate headquarters cares much if you succeed or fail and, as you can imagine, there are always some who are rooting that you crash and burn. Regardless of any promises made during the recruiting full-court press, once you're on board, you're on your own in a lot of ways. It's up to you to succeed or fail. If you look as if you might succeed, you'll probably get a little more love from your broker and, if you're lucky, an experienced agent might take you under his or her wing. But real estate agents are naturally competitive and if they don't see any personal benefit to helping you out, they won't.

> **BROKER**
>
> *When I reference "your broker" or "the broker," I am referring to the boss at your real estate firm. He/she is ultimately responsible for ensuring that you are trained and supervised and should be available to answer questions for you. He/she may or may not sell real estate along with managing the office. I also occasionally use the term "broker" to refer to other real estate agents as this is our proper title in Colorado.*

That said, you can find boutique offices that are more rah-rah and team-oriented and, if you're the type of person who needs the support of a team, you might try to search these out. I worked at one of these boutique firms for two years—lots of office activities—handing out candy at Halloween, pictures with Santa at Christmas, weekly office meetings, etc. All the agents in the office were good friends and frequently socialized together outside of work.

At this office, on Wednesdays (broker open house day), all the agents would travel around together to the open houses for the free lunches. Often they wouldn't get back to their desks (and their phone calls) until mid-afternoon. Friday evenings were frequently spent together at happy hours and every month at least one agent had a little soiree for the other agents in the office and their spouses.

As you may have noticed by my use of "they" in the preceding paragraph, I did not participate. To me, it was crazy to spend what little free time I might have socializing with other real estate agents—how much business are they going to send my way? This is a business of constant prospecting, and your friends should be your primary source of good referrals. Any social activity you do should be a potential source of business, even if you don't overtly prospect.

If you must, have one or two friends in the business to brainstorm and commiserate with, but don't make your colleagues your main source of friends. There are only so many hours in the day; don't waste good prospecting time hanging out with the competition.

Was I popular at this rah-rah office? What do you think?

Did it bother me? Sometimes.

But, who do you think was the top producing agent?

▪ *Myth #7*

You Shouldn't Ever Discount Your Fee

I will discuss fee negotiation in depth later in the book, but, contrary to popular opinion, I think you can find perfectly acceptable reasons to discount your fee. And not just because you capitulate to the pressure of the seller at your listing presentation. I think discounting your services for your friends and past clients is a fine idea, as is offering a deep discount while you're learning the business.

That said, you actually can avoid any discussion of fee negotiation, which is often the most painful part of your listing presentation. (I'll show you how in Chapter Nine.) When you should be discussing the price of the home, your proposed marketing activities and your enthusiasm for the property, instead you're battling with the seller over your commission percentage. This is not the way to build trust or rapport between you and your seller, which will be critical during the process of marketing and selling her home.

But anyway, don't get all snotty about reducing your fee in the right situation. There's plenty of money to go around, so don't be greedy!

Some Truths

Successful real estate agents can make big bucks. For a career that requires only a month or two of education, the rewards can be tremendous. But be aware of the reasons the economy supports paying real estate agents such high fees.

One of them is that you are not a nine to fiver. You are available! Most of the world works nine-to-five; therefore, as a service provider (that's what you are), you need to be available when it is convenient for your clients.

Don't get me started on those real estate agents and real estate coaches who refer to themselves in the same context with CPA's and attorneys. Such as... "You wouldn't call your CPA at 7:00 on Sunday evening..." or "You wouldn't try to negotiate your fee with your attorney, would you?" Get over it, people.

TIRADE ALERT!

We are real estate agents, not CPA's. Compare the education and licensing required to get your JD, MD or CPA against the month or two you spend in real estate school learning how to pass a one-hour test. If I were going to be so arrogant as to compare myself to one of these professionals, I would more likely use an obstetrician as a comparison. When the baby is ready to come out, the doctor goes to work. Even at 7:00 on Sunday evenings.

The good news is that successful real estate agents can make as much as or more than these higher qualified professionals, but with some trade-offs.

First, you need to be available to your clients when it's convenient to them, not you. Sure, they'll take time off from their work-day to visit their attorney, but they may not do it for their real estate agent. If you insist on working M-F 9:00 to 5:00, believe me, someone else working evenings and weekends would be happy to take your prospects. *And they will.*

Second, you agree to be paid on contingency. You take the risk every day that the work you do will not be compensated. More Risk = More $Reward$. Less Risk = Less $Reward$. Not too many professions work with no guarantee of payment. Therefore, you can justify higher fees upon success. If you could convince your clients to pay you hourly (good luck), you could charge a reasonable hourly fee and would probably make much less money per transaction. Overall, you might come out ahead though.

So remember that the next time you get a $10,000 paycheck for, say, ten hours of work—that $10,000 is also paying for those flaky buyer clients who run you around and mysteriously disappear. It doesn't mean that you and your services are worth $1,000/hour.

We real estate agents get spoiled by our big paychecks. We actually think we earned that $10,000 check during that specific transaction. Even if a client put you through the wringer for a year, it's not likely you spent more than 50 hours on his transaction. And, $200 an hour is pretty good pay for anyone.

My personal mantra is that "I sell real estate every day. Sometimes I even get paid for it!" It keeps me sane!

So before you get hostile toward prospects who never take you to a closing, realize that real estate fees are structured to pay you for that "wasted" time. Of course, the better your closing ratio, the less you have to worry about such things, but in your first year(s) you will "waste" a lot of time on unproductive people. But, as we will see later, there is no such thing as wasting your time in your rookie year.

FIRST THINGS FIRST
SOME THOUGHTS ON CHOOSING YOUR OFFICE

If you haven't yet selected a real estate office to bless with your presence, here are some ideas to ponder.

Be assured that there is a place for you. If you are marginally presentable and have a pulse (most days), a real estate office will "hire" you. In fact, the interview process is more about you interviewing them, rather than the other way around. Big Name companies specialize in recruiting and training new agents fresh out of school and will be happy to talk with you. You might even feel a little flattered at their attention and persuasive recruiting tactics!

That said, smaller boutique companies don't typically recruit rookie agents. If they do, they tend to be quite selective, so if you prefer to start your career at a boutique firm, you may have to actually sell yourself to the broker. Brokerages in small towns or resort communities may also be a little harder to break into than those in a metropolitan area.

When I first got my license, I was told that the urban brokers (where I wanted to work) wouldn't even talk to brand new licensees. Not being overly bold, I didn't push the issue, I just interviewed in the suburbs and received "offers" from every suburban company I talked to. I chose to work in a Big Name office in the foothills outside of Denver because it sounded glamorous to sell mountain real estate. Never mind that I knew nothing about mountain real estate, or cared, really. I couldn't relate to the other brokers in the office or to any of the prospects I gathered who wanted a mountain lifestyle. I was a city girl and I understood city dwellers.

After nine months, I transferred to another office in a suburb of Denver. That was an even worse fit for me; while I didn't really connect with mountain buyers, I was utterly baffled by suburban ones! Tri-level homes built in 1975 with popcorn ceilings just weren't my thing. Six months later, I moved again, this time to a boutique firm in central Denver. Ah, the euphoria and camaraderie of working with agents who knew the difference between a Bungalow and a Cottage, a Denver Square and a Victorian.

My point is that you should strive to work in an office that fits your personality and interests, whether it is a specific neighborhood or market, an age group, a market specialty or just general ambience. Some offices are quite formal and stuffy; others are somewhat casual or even dumpy. You'll find corporate firms to be beige, boutiques more colorful and eclectic. Opportunities for referrals and good open houses will come more naturally (and be more enjoyable) if you are working in an atmosphere that feels like home. You will probably "know" when you're in the right place. Wait for that feeling.

However, don't fret if your first office doesn't work out. It's no big deal to move and, after a year in the business, you'll have a much better idea of what you're looking for.

A Word About Splits

As you probably know, your split is the percentage of your commissions you get to keep. If you are on a 60/40 split, you keep 60%, your brokerage firm gets 40%. When you're brand new, there probably isn't a lot of room to negotiate the split and you'll drive yourself crazy trying to compare offers from different companies. Just select the company that seems to best suit your personality, your need for training and/or personalized mentoring and, of course, your budget. You can worry about negotiating a better split after you've proven yourself.

JENNIFER'S BLOG
So, You Wanna Be a Real Estate Agent?

Almost every week, I hear from a friend or friend-of-a-friend who wants to talk about "going into real estate." Is now a good time? Is it hard work? Can I do it part time? How quickly can I make money? Should I work as an assistant first?

Successfully selling real estate IS hard—some recent estimates quote the first year drop-out rate as high as 95%. But for those who make it through that painful first year (or two), it can be a dream job. The potential for financial reward is unlimited and eventually you can choose your own hours and take time off whenever you want. Selling real estate can give you the lifestyle you always dreamed of, as long as you're willing to devote several years of hard work to building your business.

One of the best-known perks to being in the business is the opportunity to purchase property under market value, get a paid a commission for doing so and eliminate the majority of the fees associated with the sale of your investment property. However, (in my humble opinion) it's a waste of time to get your real estate license for the sole purpose of buying investment real estate unless you have an ongoing, reliable source of under-market properties other than the MLS. The best deals are discovered during the course of your regular business day, listing homes, showing buyers and chatting with prospects. Just having a real estate license doesn't automatically deliver Great Deals to your in-box, unfortunately.

If I had to sum up in one word what I think it takes to succeed as a new real estate agent, I'd pick ENTHUSIASM. You must be excited about your new career, constantly looking for opportunities to enlarge your circle of friends, develop your market knowledge and dive into unfamiliar situations. When the phone rings at 7 p.m. on a Sunday evening, you jump up to answer it. If a client wants to look at homes during the Super Bowl, you're there. You might even consider canceling your vacation to accommodate a new client. (No, you don't have to actually cancel it, but the thought crosses your mind.)

In other words, Real Estate is your life. Don't worry, it won't be this way forever, but when you're starting out in a business with an 80% failure rate, you need to be THIS excited and THIS committed. Go Get 'em! Rah Rah Rah!

■ ■ ■ ■ ■

beating the odds

First Things First
Let's get the bad news out of the way

The failure rate for rookie agents is staggering. You probably already know that. Depending on whom you talk to, drop-out rates range from 70% to 95%. It's common for first-year agents to work for several months (as in, more than two) before seeing a paycheck. The first year can be brutal. Amazingly discouraging. Unbelievably expensive.

Still with me?

Good. It doesn't have to be that way. Just because a lot of people fail doesn't mean you will. Just the fact that you're reading this book shows you have a lot more gumption than, well, 70% to 95% of the other new agents out there! The reasons for rookie failure are many and varied, but we don't care about that. Why dwell on the reasons someone fails? NO! Let's "dwell" on the reasons agents succeed...and make it past their critical rookie year.

Success in a real estate career is a beautiful thing. This career offers unlimited potential for financial reward, a flexible schedule (eventually) and, frankly, tons of fun (most of the time). Yes, you'll pay your dues and you'll work your backside off, but you will be rewarded for your efforts.

But that's a ways off. Let's talk about now. What you, as a real estate rookie, can do today to ensure your success .

ENTHUSIASM

You must have enthusiasm to succeed in real estate. It's so easy to procrastinate when you are self-employed—or to sleep late every day if you're so inclined. Prospecting and previewing seem thankless sometimes.

When I was new in real estate, I had it—enthusiasm, that is. I did open houses every weekend, took names and made cookies. I would work with any buyer, regardless of his motivation or time frame. I even offered to show relocating renters around town just in case they might buy a house someday. I marketed my listings in every imaginable venue–newspapers, mass mailings, postcards and city-wide brochure distribution.

I answered the phone at all hours of the day or night. I worked seven days a week. I checked voicemail during vacation and returned business calls from a hot, noisy street in Mexico.

I'm not saying that these were all smart things to do. I spent a lot of money unnecessarily and destroyed my marriage in the process. But to succeed in this tough business you need to be excited about your new career, nearly to the point of fanaticism.

I once interviewed a licensee right out of real estate school who announced to me that he intended to take every Sunday and Monday off. Fair enough. But then I realized that he meant he wouldn't even answer his phone on his days off, at the risk of losing potential customers. After several years in real estate, I got to the point where I was willing to risk losing customers for the sake of a mental health day, but in my first year? No way. I lived for phone calls from potential clients. I literally did cartwheels a few times when I got off the phone with a new buyer or a referral. I got a little thrill every time my pager went off; I couldn't wait to see who had called. I still feel that way most of the time.

That new agent didn't make it in real estate—he quit within the year. He probably could have been a great agent, but his heart just wasn't in it.

If your lifestyle doesn't accommodate a 24/7 availability to your clients, you can still succeed. You can always find people willing to work harder than you, regardless of what field you are in. And guess what? They may be more successful financially than you, and that's fair. Life is about priorities and compromises. You can't have it all and do any of it exceptionally well.

That said, early in your real estate career you really do need to be committed to building your expertise and business. Remember the 70% to 95% failure rate for first year agents? An awful lot of those failures are likely competent people who aren't prepared for the overwhelming demands of a new real estate career.

Just think about it.

A $7,000 Phone Call

Back to the issue of 24/7...as part of my research for this book, I read several "How to Succeed in Real Estate" books. I found that I disagreed with much of the advice I found, especially the advice to "work regular hours." As in, don't take calls after 6 p.m., don't work seven days a week, don't drop everything to meet your client in 15 minutes.

Okay, sure, follow that advice if you have plenty of money, plenty of experience and no enthusiasm for your career. Are you telling me that you aren't dying for the phone to ring? If you aren't, you may be in the wrong business.

If you're a rookie agent, you probably aren't all that busy. At least, you aren't busy doing activities that are bringing in a paycheck in the next 30 days. When the phone rings and a prospect wants something from you, you better respond.

One Sunday evening I was putting dinner on the table for my husband and his parents. My cell phone rang. I love my job, so it didn't occur to me not to answer it. Turns out it was a buyer I had worked with six months earlier who hadn't bought anything. She and her husband were open-housing that afternoon and stumbled upon a home they had to have. And, God bless 'em, they called me! If I hadn't answered the phone, their next call would have been to the agent holding the open house and I never would have known.

I dropped everything, wrote up the offer, and made $7,000 because I answered the phone. This happens, a lot. If your lifestyle doesn't allow you to be this responsive, maybe now isn't the time for you to go into real estate. However, when you're real successful, several years down the line, you may decide your personal life can't take being on call 24/7. At that point, it may be acceptable to forego a $7,000 commission, but in the beginning, I assume it would break your heart to miss a call like this.

Do you get excited when the phone rings?

LOVE & THE REAL ESTATE AGENT

You may have heard that real estate agents have a higher than normal divorce rate. Why?

This career can take over your life, physically, financially and emotionally. Physically, you will be Missing-in-Action frequently, often without notice. Financially, you may be dipping into the family nest-egg to keep your business afloat, without much to show for your efforts. Emotionally, oh my. The emotional havoc a new real estate career can wreak in your life can't be overstated. You will be on a crazy roller-coaster ride, most of the time. There are incredible highs and devastating lows...all in the same day.

If you are married or otherwise romantically entangled, please don't underestimate the effect your career will have on your relationship. Maybe it will be the best thing that ever happened to you. Maybe not. But your relationship WILL change. Your spouse or significant other will need to accept that the love of his or her life is spending time alone with other people, sometimes in emotionally charged situations. That they will often appear to place these other people and their needs above the needs of the family. That they will be testy, teary and tardy. They will work late, they will work early, they will work on vacation. They may even threaten to cancel a vacation every once in a while!

If you jump into real estate full-time, your spouse or significant other may be footing the bills for you. Don't forget to acknowledge and be appreciative of this fact. Often. Discuss it up front so that no one is blind-sided three months down the line. Don't assume that your partner is happily paying the bills—resentment can build up fast, especially if your new career is straining the relationship in other ways.

Do your best to put your family at the top of your priority list, but know that they won't always stay there. When you are building a new business, any business, you need to be fanatically obsessed with the success of that business. And, unfortunately, something will have to give. You simply can't have it all and do any of it exceptionally well. That's just a fact.

If your family does not fully support your commitment to sell real estate, you may have a big decision to make. Only you can make the best decision for your situation, but just know that without your family's support, you will probably be miserable most of the time. And a miserable real estate agent won't be a real estate agent for long.

The good news is that after a few crazy years, you may very well be able to control your time, your energy, your finances and your emotions much better than you can at first. In fact, if you play it smart, you can create a life for you and your family that the rest of the world will envy.

Full-time or Part-time?

Back in my day (way back before the days of Internet, email and the sub-prime mortgage crisis), no one sold real estate part-time. At least, no one I knew. It never occurred to me, not even for a second, to keep my day job when I began my new career.

And no, there was no more guarantee of success back then than there is now. The grim failure rates and statistics you see bandied about today were not much different back then, and most new real estate agents failed, just as they do today.

But for some reason, the current trend among new agents is to ease into a real estate career by fitting real estate in around their "real" job. Hmmmmm.

I think this is a lousy idea. In my never-to-be-humble opinion, I think you ought to either jump into your real estate career full throttle or WAIT until you can.

I know this opinion is unpopular. I know because whenever I've expressed it in a public forum I've been called elitist, unrealistic and idealistic. And those comments came from people who liked me.☺

Let's talk about the reasons someone might become a PT real estate agent... Um...okay, only one reason comes to mind. Money. Not enough of it.

I can't think of any other reason someone would start a new career and only attack it half-assed (or less!)

This is a tough business; we all know that. So, if you are considering entering a business in which 70% or more don't make it through the first year, the odds are very much against your chances of succeeding. And you think that giving it less than your all is going to improve those odds?

The common song I hear when agents insist on going part-time is a whining, "Well, it would be NICE if I could do it full-time, but not EVERYONE has that luxury!"

Fair enough.

Then, maybe, just maybe, this isn't the right time. Just because selling real estate is your dream doesn't mean that you are entitled to succeed if you aren't ready. Some dreams may just have to wait. Patience, grasshopper!

But enough ranting and raving (maybe). Here are some solid reasons part-time is not nearly as cool as full-time:

1.   Being part-time screams to your friends, prospects and clients that you aren't successful enough to do it full-time. And who wants to work with an unsuccessful real estate agent?

2.   Being part-time requires you to be oh-so-efficient with your time. This sounds like a good thing, but it's not. In the course of learning to be a good real estate agent, you need to be able to risk "wasting" your time. For example, let's say you get a floor call from a marginally qualified buyer. If you're part-time, you might be tempted (or forced) to turn him away. If you're full-time, you're delighted for the opportunity to practice your craft, regardless of the potential for a paycheck. But I guarantee you, whether or not you get paid for running around with this buyer, the learning experience will be worth every "wasted" minute. And who knows, this buyer could end up being your biggest referral source.

But as a part-time agent who doesn't have time to mess around, you'll never know.

3.   I don't see how a new part-time agent can truly serve her clients when she doesn't have the time to learn her craft. When I was new, everything I did took me five times as long to do as it should have because I had a huge learning curve to climb over. I worked very hard (full-time) to learn my market, to master my systems, to know my contracts inside and out, to develop my team

of service providers and oh, yes, to answer my phone every time my clients called…or to return their calls within five minutes.

4.   Your paying clients expect and deserve your full attention. Especially when you're new and, c'mon, admit it, you don't know what you're doing. When you go on your first listing appointment, you SHOULD have spent the previous 48 hours straight preparing your market analysis. Your fear of failure and embarrassment should motivate you to go through the comparable market data with a fine toothed comb. A part-time agent doesn't have the time or energy for this.

Your buyer needs an agent who is as enthusiastic about his house-hunt as he is. He deserves an agent who previews like a madman to find just the right house the day it hits the market. An agent who is willing and able to hold the buyer's hand through the painful inspection. An agent who can drop everything and spend five hours making phone calls when a last-minute crisis threatens your buyer's closing.

5.   The agent on the other side of the deal expects and deserves your attention. She doesn't want to do your job for you just because you're at your "real" job and can't get away. And remember, you're making her look bad to her clients when she can't reach you to get a question answered or a problem resolved.

6.   Selling real estate is a constant learning experience. Even full-time, experienced agents learn something new with every sale or listing. If you're only selling four or five houses a year because you're part-time, you're missing out on a lot of on-the-job training. It doesn't matter how smart, how motivated or how charming you are, you'll never be as qualified as a good full-time agent.

(Note I said "good." There are plenty of bad full-time agents and you may very well be more qualified than some of them).

7.   In both of your careers, if something goes wrong, it's going to be blamed on your dual-life. Perhaps with good reason.

Again, I know my opinion is unpopular. But I also know how hard I worked in my first five years, and I can't imagine succeeding in (or even enjoying) this career without devoting my heart and soul to it.

So, here's an alternate plan. If you want to sell real estate and you want to succeed...work your backside off for the next year doing something else and save some money. Work two or even three jobs that guarantee you a paycheck and put that money away. After all, that's what you're talking about doing anyway, right? Working two jobs? If you think building a real estate business is easier than, say, waiting tables at night, you're mistaken. At least waiting tables guarantees you $3/hour with no out-of-pocket costs!

Then, hit your new career with guns blazing. ALL your energy. ALL your enthusiasm. ALL your attention. You'll be glad you did, I promise.

JENNIFER'S BLOG
I'm New! Don't Waste My Time!

We old fogies (those of us with more than a year of experience) like to advise the newbies in our lives on how to work efficiently and productively and gawd forbid—how not to WASTE TIME!

What are some "time-wasters" in our business?

How about:

1. Working with an unqualified buyer?
2. Talking to renters
3. Showing a listing to an already-represented buyer (who calls off the yard sign)
4. Preparing a CMA for a seller who wants to move "sometime next year"
5. Having lunch with friends who already know lots of real estate agents
6. Helping an acquaintance appeal her tax assessment

Well, in this old fogie's humble opinion, there's NO SUCH THING as wasting time in your first year if you're doing something that:

1. Puts you in front of a warm body and/or
2. Teaches you about the real estate market

Let's take example #3—Showing an office listing to an already-represented buyer.

Here's the scenario. You're sitting on floor time twiddling your thumbs, or maybe working up the nerve to call a few FSBO's. The phone rings. You find yourself talking with a buyer who is sitting out in front of one of your office's listings. He wants to see it right away. He tells you he already has a buyer agent, but he can't seem to track him down today. He's just so busy, y'know. So...can YOU show it to him?

Option I   Tell the "buyer" in no uncertain terms that you don't work for free and he needs to wait for his own agent!

Option II   Cheerfully say, "Sure! Give me some time to notify the owner and I'll meet you there in 30 minutes! What's your phone number in case there's a problem?"

Let's say you select Option I. Here's what you accomplished:

You're still sitting at your desk, twiddling your thumbs, but by gawd, you didn't waste your time. And, oh yeah, you probably confirmed the buyer's opinion that real estate agents are jerks.

Conversely, with Option II, you:

• Practiced showing homes and building rapport with strangers

• Possibly learned just a little more about the market

• Met someone who just might end up being your biggest referral source (you never know)

• Met someone who just might be the love of your life (you never know!)

• Got your arse off the chair and OUT INTO THE WORLD

• Improved, just a little, the public's perception of real estate agents

• And maybe, just maybe…you'll get yourself a client if the buyer decides you're way cooler than his missing-in-action agent.

Sounds like a no-brainer to me. Get off your butt and go waste some time!

COMPETENCE…BEGETS CONFIDENCE…

One of my many real estate mantras is: Competence…gives you Confidence.

Many new agents ask how they can "demonstrate confidence" with their prospects. The answer is quite simple, actually…yet also very complicated.

As a reader of Sell with Soul, I suspect you are not a blow-'em-away-with-your-sales-pitch kinda guy or gal. You aren't an aggressive, hard-core salesperson who can sell ice to Eskimos. And you aren't going to be able to fake a confident attitude!

But you will absolutely, positively need a confident attitude to attract customers and clients to you. So, what's a soulful rookie to do?

The only way to gain true self-confidence is to be good at your job. Period. True self-confidence is not something you can learn. Either you are confident... or you aren't. As you know, I'm an introvert and not a natural horn-blower, but get me talking about properly pricing a home for market or negotiating a tough inspection and you'll think I'm the most confident person on the planet. Why? Because I know my stuff.

Self-confidence as a salesperson is not about meditation, daily affirmations or rev-you-up motivation seminars and CDs. It's about having something to be confident about. And...it's a BLAST to be really good at what you do!

That's my goal for you. Let's get you there!

YOUR ELEVATOR SPEECH

The agent asks... "What can I tell people about myself in 30 seconds that will make them want to work with me?"

That's a tough one. I've seen some pretty creative answers. Most answers center around bragging about one's expertise, one's helpful nature and one's successes.

Hmmmm.

I'm trying to think of a time someone bragged to me about themselves and I was so impressed I asked for their business card. Can't think of one. We human beings tend to be contrarians and will argue (at least mentally) with just about anything. Tell me how great you are, and I'm already thinking of reasons to disagree with you.

So, what do you say to someone you just met to motivate them to want to know more about you?

Try this secret phrase.

"I'm a real estate agent!"

If you announce it with your shoulders back and a big smile on your face, like being a real estate agent is the coolest job in the whole world...it's magnetic. People will be irresistibly drawn to you and can't help but want to know more about you.

Unfortunately, it doesn't work if you fake it. If you don't love your job and don't think it's the coolest in the world...no one else will either.

But if you do love your job and think you're pretty darn good at it...try the secret phrase a few times and let me know how it goes.

SUCCESS OR FAILURE...
IT'S NOT THE CIRCUMSTANCES, IT'S YOU!

Excerpted from
"Don't Sweat the Small Stuff About Money" by Richard Carlson, Ph.D. [1]

It's extremely rare to find a successful person who whines, complains, and frets about her circumstances. This is despite the fact that she may have overcome great obstacles to achieve her level of success. On the other hand, it's extremely common for struggling individuals to continually blame their circumstances for their lack of joy and abundance. The real question is: What came first—the attitude or the success? The answer, in virtually all cases, is that the winning, positive attitude came first, followed by a lifetime of abundance.

Your circumstances are what they are; they were what they were...it's time to get over them and move on.

You'll find that life will be a lot easier and much more fun when you make the decision to drop your complaining. All it does is make you feel sorry for yourself—sad, angry, victimized, suspicious and / or self righteous. When you argue for your limitations, your thoughts and words merely get in your way and greatly interfere with your ability to create. With complaining out of the way, you'll create the space for an explosion of creativity and brilliance. You'll be able to be more focused and oriented to the present moment. Instead of focusing on problems, you'll begin to see solutions. Instead of maintaining an 'I can't' attitude, you'll quickly develop a more positive vision for yourself.

---

1   Richard Carlson, Ph.D., Don't Sweat the Small Stuff About Money, Hyperion, 1997 & 2001, page 75

There is a lot of doom, gloom and negativity in the world of real estate sales these days. And with reason, it's a scary place to be right now! It's hard for someone to take the plunge into this career when everything you hear tells you that you must be crazy. I'm proud of you for moving ahead. That optimism will serve you well.

I have been accused of being a Rah-Rah, that is, someone who looks at the world thru rose-colored glasses and thinks that if you have a great attitude, things will always work out fine.

Well, yeah, sorta.

I live my life by the Law of Attraction, which states that you bring into your life what you focus on. So if you focus on your worries, you'll bring more in your life to worry about! Conversely, if you focus on the happiness you feel when things go your way, you'll attract more things to be happy about.

That's a simplistic explanation, of course. You'll find a lot of subtle references to the Law of Attraction scattered throughout the Sell with Soul philosophy, although I never knew until recently that my philosophy had a name!

But anyway, let's talk about how your attitude can make the difference between success and failure.

If a real estate agent, new or otherwise, doesn't believe he will succeed, he won't. Period. It doesn't matter how good or dismal the market is, it doesn't matter how attentive or utterly absent your managing broker is, it doesn't matter how many other agents belong to your MLS board, if you suspect you might fail, you probably will.

Many new agents blame their lack of success on the market. Makes sense, doesn't it? If the market is so awful, if buyers can't get loans and sellers are upside down in their mortgages, doesn't it sound reasonable that this will affect the success ratios of people who sell real estate?

Maybe, maybe not.

Even in the booming markets, agents failed every day—in similar numbers as today. I remember when I started in 1996, I was told that over 70% fail in this business. Did it scare me? Heck no. It NEVER occurred to me that I would fail. Truly—it never crossed my mind. Was the market good? Yep, it was great.

But I didn't know that. I didn't know the difference between a good market and a bad market. And it wouldn't have mattered to me.

Do you want a guarantee?

Well, here's one. While a great attitude will not guarantee your success, a negative attitude will almost certainly guarantee your failure.

In order to succeed, you'll need to work hard, work smart and bounce back quickly from disappointments. Throw a little luck and a great attitude in the mix and I'll guarantee you a great shot at a wildly successful career selling real estate.

If You're New with More Time than Money...
By Janie Coffey, Papillon Real Estate, LLC

So, you are new to real estate and it is just starting to sink in that YOU have to build YOUR business. The whole "business development" and "lead generation" thing didn't even register with you when you so excitedly signed up for your classes and took your test. Likely, it might not have really crossed your mind until you had passed the test, signed up with a broker and had your first set of business cards in your hand.

And now what?

You are beginning to realize, "Wow, being a real estate agent is expensive!"

And it certainly can be; postcards, ads, mailers, bus benches, pens, gadgets, gimmicks, you name it, we agents love our marketing stuff. But in the beginning, it might not be practical for your present pocketbook.

So what's a newbie to do?

In my very first GRI class, I had a teacher who was older than dirt, and he KNEW this business. His line was simple, "You have to have the time or the money, or the time AND the money, but must have at least one."

Here are some suggestions for those of you who don't have the money, but have the time.

Find out if your Real Estate Board provides you with a free website. It might not be perfect, but for getting your feet off the ground, Free is Good! It will also give you time to figure out what you want out of your website, before you commit your dollars.

Search out other websites that have content similar to yours and ask them to provide a link to your site in exchange for a reciprocal link back to their site. Keep a list of whom you have requested this from, check their sites and remind if necessary.

Write articles for the local paper about your farm area and market stats. Diligently be on the lookout for opportunities to be published. Try to become a guest feature writer. Look for opportunities in your local and state trade websites and publications.

Hand out 100 cards a week! First, create a great card. It can be pretty, it can be colorful, it can be funny; just strive to have a card that inspires someone to say "Wow, that's a great card!" when you hand it to them.

Write to local probate attorneys, mortgage brokers and other affiliated service providers about your services.

Leave your business cards at local businesses on the bulletin boards—always carry a ton of them and push pins; there are lots of places that allow this, including grocery stores, Home Depot, pet stores, etc.

Network, Network, Network—get out there and be seen! Go to anything and everything where you are in front of people who make up your target client base. Get to know them, take lots of cards. Be helpful, be friendly.

Driving for Dollars—spend a day or two a week just driving around your area, get to know what is on the market, who the movers and shakers are, what's moving, what's not moving. Just be out there.

Floor time—if your brokerage offers it, USE it! Here is an opportunity every day to talk to potential new clients!

These might not all resonate with you, but more than a few should. Pick some and really work them. Money certainly helps to kick-start your business building, but if you have the time, energy and passion, you can do just as well on a lean (or virtually non-existent) marketing budget.

■ ■ ■ ■ ■

Chapter Four

let's get this party started
your first week

So Much to Do, So Little Time...

To Begin...at the Beginning

Your first week as a Licensed Real Estate Agent will be busy! Your second week as a Licensed Real Estate Agent will be busy! So will your third and fourth weeks. Then it will get crazy. Hopefully for many years to come.

Seriously, you need to be crazy-busy right away to get you focused, build your momentum and strengthen your organizational skills. When you're self-employed, especially if you've never been self-employed before, it's easy to procrastinate.

So, no procrastinating! Let's talk about what you need to be doing in those first seven days.

> Set up your phone, fax and e-mail.
> Start learning your systems.
> Schedule a photo session.
> Start building your SOI database.
> Consider your announcement strategy.
> Learn about previewing.

Just Because You're New...
by Ashley Drake Gephart

Just because you're new, doesn't mean you have to look it.

When I was starting out, I showed amazing confidence and was never once asked how much experience I had. But to have confidence, you need to have knowledge.

Know your market

Preview everything in your area. Go on tours or go on your own—just preview. Don't just preview your own office's listings, but preview other listings as well. If your town is big, just focus on a small section. Previewing around where you live is key, and I will explain more about why in a bit.

Hot Sheets

Read them daily. Know what home prices actually go under contract and what prices end up expired. What is the average DOM or price per sq. ft.? If someone asks you what homes are selling for in, say, Blue Jupiter, you can respond, "The average sale price is $135 a sq. ft." Boom! No hesitation on your part.

Here is where focusing on the area where you live is good. You will be at the store, post office, library, school, soccer game, etc., and someone will ask about prices. Make sure you know your market. You live there so you should know it without having to look it up.

Listing Presentations

Practice your listing presentation. Try it with a flip chart, booklet, laptop or from memory. If something just doesn't feel right, change it until it flows smoothly. Practice on your partner, family, a colleague, the kids, or the cat. You don't want to practice on the homeowner.

Buyer Consultations

Again, practice. Try different styles of gathering the information you need to find your buyer the best home. Interview them using a checklist, ask about their lifestyle, and take free-form notes. Have a buyers book with information about mortgages, utilities, escrow, FAQs, etc. Again, practice on your family, a colleague, or the kids. The cat might not be responsive enough for this one, though. Find a style that works for you and then practice it.

Contracts

Study them thoroughly. I read my contracts so that I can summarize the key points on each page without looking at them. Have a copy of all the basic forms (listing contract, purchase agreement, sellers disclosure, lead paint, etc.) everywhere. Keep a set in your day planner, a copy on your PDA, and a set in the car and your purse or briefcase. Read them whenever you are waiting at an appointment, when it's slow during an open house, or while the kids are in ballet. Read them every day. Know them!

Practice filling them out. Print out an MLS sheet and write an offer on it. Then write the listing contract for it as well. Have someone in your office look it over for you. Do this once a week until you're comfortable with the forms.

When a new form comes out or one gets updated—no matter how long you have been in the business—study it and practice filling it out.

Net outs

After filling out the purchase agreement and listing agreement on the house you pulled from the MLS, do a net out for both the seller and the buyer. Do these by hand. You will not always have access to a computer for using one of the title companies' online calculators. You need to be able to do these on the kitchen counter of a vacant house while filling out the purchase agreement.

Open Houses

Go visit open houses and see how other agents are doing them. Some will be very bad and some will be superb. You will learn something from each one. Go to several on one weekend, making sure to visit different agencies.

Now you can take this experience to make your open houses superb, and, from seeing others, you will gain a level of confidence by doing your own.

With enough practice, you will come across as the knowledgeable professional agent that you now are!

A Good Real Estate Agent Shouldn't Be Hard to Find...

Perfecting Your Communication Systems

Sometimes the difference between a $7,000 paycheck and, well, no $7,000 paycheck can be as simple as an answered (or unanswered) phone call. You need a dedicated business phone with voicemail (your cell phone is fine) as well as a dedicated fax line and e-mail address.

Phones...

Don't use the office number as your primary contact number. You want to maximize the potential that you answer the phone when it rings because answering the phone makes you money. Also, you want your contact information to be portable so if you leave the company, your friends and past clients can find you.

Make sure the outgoing message on your voicemail is professional and friendly so that callers know you're excited to hear from them. Many agents have the most sour, dour, unapproachable, unfriendly outgoing message, which may just be the first (and last) impression someone has of them. Don't share your business phone line with your family, and make sure that your outgoing message announces that you're in real estate. Many times I've called real estate agents and hung up when I got their voicemail because the message didn't sound like someone who was in business. Don't risk losing even one prospect because the caller isn't sure he or she is actually calling a real estate professional.

I used to carry a pager that notified me whenever I had a new voicemail on my home office business line. As soon as the pager went off, I checked my voicemail and returned the call immediately. I'll bet I got a dozen clients this way in my first year alone. (Math Quiz! If my average sales price in 1996 was around $170,000, and my average commission percentage was 2.5%, and I sold twelve homes as a result of my pager...how much money did my pager make me?)

Since most of us work off our cell phones now, a pager is probably way too 1990's for the 21st Century real estate agent. But the theory still holds. Carrying a pager trained me to constantly check my messages and I am still obsessive about it. That's a good thing while you're striving to beat the odds in a tough career.

In short, don't count on your friends or prospects to track you down; make sure you do everything in your power to take their phone calls. Or at least return their calls within five minutes. I'm serious.

Faxes...

You need a dedicated fax line. Agents who have to race home to "turn on the fax machine," and then figure out how it works, come across as unprofessional and well...flaky. I use e-fax, which is great. My faxes are e-mailed to me, so I can pick them up from any computer. I can save them as PDF files, so it's easy to forward them on to other agents, clients, lenders or title representatives without worrying about the dreaded "fax of a fax of a fax syndrome." I don't have to have a separate phone line in the house, although I do still need a fax machine for outgoing faxes.

If you plan to use your office fax number, that's fine for now, but once you're getting some action (i.e., sales), you'll want a fax machine at home. Alas...a lot of real estate negotiation happens after you're comfortably nested at home, snuggled up in your jammies.

E-mails...

You need an e-mail address that you check frequently and isn't likely to change. I highly recommend using a "permanent" e-mail address (such as your own domain name) that isn't tied to your real estate company (such as newagent@ KellerWilliams.com). That way if you leave your first company (and chances are you will) you'll reduce the likelihood of losing potential customers after the transition.

MASTERING YOUR SYSTEMS

Let's talk about your systems. By "systems" I'm referring to the (mostly) computer-based programs that you will use on a daily basis as a real estate agent. When you don't know your systems, you won't be able to exude the confidence you need to inspire others to have confidence in you.

Your Online MLS

The first system you must learn is your online MLS. You need to understand the MLS inside and out, starting now.

I've worked in four real estate markets, and all the MLS systems were completely different. Accessing them for the first time will require the assistance of your office manager. Some MLS's require that you check out software from the local Board of Realtors®; some require you to purchase the software, some provide a free download link, others are simply accessed online with a login ID and password.

Even a half hour of training will get you started. Find out if there is additional training available, either through the local Board or the MLS vendor. You need to be intimately familiar with your MLS before you start working with buyers or sellers. You really can't call yourself a real estate agent until you are able to competently access information in the real estate market.

If your MLS isn't user-friendly, ask your broker or trainer if there are other MLS programs in addition to the standard MLS. I have three different programs I use for different purposes...one for MLS input and maintenance, one for buyers and one for seller CMAs. I just like the way each one searches for and organizes the data for my specific purposes.

The best way to familiarize yourself with the MLS is to do some practice searches. For example...

Search for:

Active Single Family Homes in your neighborhood
Price range $200,000-$235,000
Minimum # bedrooms: 3
Minimum # baths: 2
Car Storage: Garage

(Obviously, you'll need to customize your search for your market. The point is to find some homes to look at that are in a neighborhood familiar to you.)

The Tax Assessor's Database

Hopefully, your market has an accessible tax assessor database. Typically, these databases include information such as square footage of the home, lot size, assessed value, year of construction and owner name. This information is extremely helpful when preparing listing presentations and purchase offers. Ask your broker for assistance.

Your Contract Software

Another system that you'll need to learn is your contract software. Contract software is used to prepare offers, counterproposals, disclosures, amendments, etc. These documents can be handwritten, but it's much more professional to prepare them electronically.

Contract software is typically not intuitive, so you'll probably need some help. Find out if your broker will train you, or if there is training offered by your company or the software vendor. If all else fails, "hire" an experienced agent to spend an hour or two with you. Then practice, practice, practice.

You need to be able to put an offer together under pressure. That pressure may be a client sitting across the desk from you or fifteen minutes away on his way to your office. Make sure you know how to print out the offer! Do a test print to confirm that your printer is aligned properly and that if you need to change the paper size, you know how to do that. I know this sounds petty, but if you're unprepared with a client staring at you while you're struggling with the printer, you'll be a basket-case. I know, I've been there.

Practice completing, printing and explaining your contracts to a make believe client. Role-play the entire process a few times (preferably in the privacy of your own home!). Practice talking with your client while filling in the blanks. "How would you like your name to read?" "What closing date works for you? How about the 29th?" "Do you want to ask for the refrigerator?"

After you've completed the offer with your "client," print it out, practice putting it in the proper order, and go through it carefully to make sure you filled in all the blanks. Note all the places your buyer will need to initial and sign. Practice explaining the difficult provisions (loan approval, inspection, etc.). Don't forget to run through the agency disclosure and/or agreement and any other required disclosures.

If you are ever offered the opportunity to watch another agent prepare and explain a contract for a real client, take advantage of it. As many times as you can.

YOUR REAL ESTATE FACE

You really should consider having your photo on your business card. It doesn't have to be stuffy though—in fact, the more attractive and distinctive your photo is, the more likely someone will be to keep it. A professionally-designed caricature can be very effective, although don't do it if it doesn't suit your personality. You can have your photos professionally done or you can have a friend take them with a high quality digital camera.

If you opt for the first, make sure your photos will be delivered to you digitally. You probably don't need any hard copies at all. If you want to try the second option, make sure to take lots and lots of photos, on your camera's highest resolution, from different angles and distances, with a few different outfits. All my photos from the last four years were taken in the comfort of my own home.

Make sure the picture you select is one you're proud of. Throughout my career, I had several photos taken, some of which I hated. Believe it or not, I hesitated to give out my business card because I was embarrassed about the picture!

BUILDING YOUR SPHERE OF INFLUENCE

In Chapter Five we'll talk extensively about generating business and referrals from your sphere of influence (or SOI, which is a fancy term for the people who know you). For a new agent in a hurry to earn a paycheck, your SOI is almost always the quickest way to get there.

One of the first assignments your new broker will give you is to make a list of everyone you know. That's good advice. G'ahead and do that.

Find a quiet place with plenty of room to spread out. You will need a notebook or legal pad and pen, your address book and your computer.

Begin by making a list of everyone you know, off the top of your head. Don't pre-edit the list—just start writing down names. Every name you can think of. It's okay if you don't know or can't remember last names; the goal is to open your mind.

Now go through your address book. Miss anyone? Add them to the list.

Go through your e-mail address book. You should find lots more names for your list here. If you have a current e-mail address for someone, that's better than a last name or even a physical address.

Do you have a stash of (other people's) business cards somewhere? Go through them. Add more names.

How about your: spouse's family, dog-groomer, insurance agent, accountant, babysitter's parents, house cleaner, neighbors, renters, landlord, lawn care guy, pest control guy, match.com contacts, kids' kindergarten teacher, hair stylist, massage therapist, webmaster, acupuncturist, pastor, rabbi, Spanish tutor, chiropractor...

Don't forget everyone you worked with at your last job and the job before that.

Did you meet some nice people at the pool party you went to last week? Call up the host and get their names and phone numbers.

An important part of this exercise is to train your mind to always be in SOI-building mode. To make you constantly, even obsessively, aware of the people you meet in your daily routine. It will become second nature soon, but for now, consciously make it your obsession.

Try to add three names to this list every day for the next two weeks. The names can be people you already know whom you forgot about or people you meet in your day-to-day wanderings.

You will need to put your SOI list in your computer—I use Top Producer, but many other programs are available. At some point in the near future you will need to commit to some sort of program to keep track of your contacts. We'll discuss this more in Chapter Fourteen.

Before I was in real estate, I only had a few friends, by choice, I liked to believe. I've just never been the type to need a lot of people around me. As you know, I'm an introvert and was reluctant to impose my friendship on anyone. Asking a friend or client out for drinks took a lot of courage for me. In fact, I was reprimanded several times in my last "real" job because too many of my clients complained that I didn't socialize with them.

My point is that I was too introverted to aggressively turn acquaintances into friends. As soon as I got my real estate license, that changed. Call me opportunistic, but I began to see friendships in a whole new light. Instead of shying away from social opportunities, I began to seek them out and nurture them. It was a life-changing realization for me. I still remember the amazement I felt when I invited some new (!) friends over for Thanksgiving dinner and they happily accepted. And actually showed up!

So, if you're an introvert like me, real estate can help you be more social. If you're already a people-person, you'll just need to train yourself to always be in SOI-building mode. You'll be amazed how quickly your list will grow to 100, 200, even 300 names. Don't let this list get stale and outdated. Make a promise to yourself to keep it current and it will be like gold to you.

YOUR "I'M IN REAL ESTATE!" ANNOUNCEMENT STRATEGY

JENNIFER'S $0.02...

Even though I am including this topic in the chapter about "Your First Week," I'd like to advise you to wait a few weeks before sending out any sort of communication to your sphere of influence (SOI) about your venture into real estate. It is prudent to wait until you feel a little more comfortable in your real estate agent skin before you go looking for business. Believe me, in a few weeks, you'll know so much more than you do today and will be much better able to handle any leads that come in as a result of your announcement. I'd hate to see you blow it with the people you know because you don't yet know your way around the MLS or understand how to set showings.

The tried and true method of announcing your new career is with a pre-printed and usually dorky-looking announcement card you order through your company or, if you're more ambitious, a "personal" letter to everyone you know telling them all about your new career.

I have a strong aversion to these cards and letters. To me, they scream, "I'm brand new and have no clue what I'm doing yet. Please, please, please call me!" These announcements are also fairly expensive and labor-intensive to send out, and you're not offering anything interesting with the letter or card, it's likely to be tossed into the trash.

Here's a typical letter:

> "Dear Friend,
> I'm pleased to announce...blah, blah, blah...my company is great...blah, blah, blah...I promise to provide the highest level of service...blah, blah, blah...please send me referrals.
>
> Love,
> *Jennifer*"

Nice, but so what?

First, just because you are new in the business, there's no good reason to announce this fact to the world. Sending out an announcement that you JUST got your real estate license and are looking for business won't give anyone much motivation to call you. Okay, well, maybe your mother and your Aunt Lulu, but no one else.

I'd rather you approach your "announcement" a little more casually. Just slide into "being in real estate." Don't make a big deal that you Just Got Your Real Estate License and are Looking for Business. Instead, simply start communicating with people you know and "remind" them that you're in real estate. Most people you know casually haven't been keeping track of your every movement, so if you're suddenly in real estate, they won't think twice about it, probably. They might even think they forgot that you were a real estate agent! And that's fine.

So instead of sending out a formal announcement, try one of these other ideas for getting the word out:

- Send out an e-mail offering your friends some promotional item or service. Don't mention that you just got your license; pretend that you've been selling real estate for a while now and "Gee, I've been so busy I've lost touch. Let's get together soon!"

- If it's holiday time, send out holiday cards with your business card enclosed. Write a "personal" note in each—"What a great year it's been! Looking forward to an even more prosperous New Year for all of us," or something like that.

• Send out a "Happy New Year" (any time of year) family newsletter with all the happenings in your life, including your venture into real estate. Don't be specific as to when your career started—just that it did start and you love it! Be sure to include your business card.

• Put together a mini-newsletter with a description of special services you "offer," as a local real estate professional. If you have a digital camera, offer to take pictures of your clients' rental properties for their online marketing. Or before-and-after shots for clients who are doing extensive remodeling. You could offer to take photos of your friends' belongings for insurance purposes. I offered my graphic design services to friends for garage sales, rental property flyers, etc. Very few people took me up on these services, but it gave me something of value to offer.

• Send thank-you cards...to anyone who helped you out that day. Some sales trainers advise sending out five thank-you cards every single day, and it's not a bad idea. Not only does this practice put you in a grateful frame of mind, it also gets your business card out there in the hands of the public.

• Open your mind...what can you mail to your friends that would have value to them, yet give you the opportunity to push your business card at them? You don't have to send the same thing to everyone—if you belong to a special interest group, clip a relevant magazine article and send out copies (along with your card and a short note). Brainstorm ideas, write them down.

Or, send out that dorky announcement. It's okay if you do that, it's just not special and it makes it kind of obvious that you're fresh off the turnip truck, so to speak.

LEARNING TO PREVIEW

My second day in real estate two experienced agents invited me to go previewing with them. I had no idea what "previewing" was, but I was up for it. Turns out it meant that we scheduled appointments to look at seven or eight homes that were on the market, toured the homes and left our business cards on the kitchen counter. Why were we previewing? Because one of the experienced agents was doing an open house that weekend in the neighborhood, so she was previewing the competition to get ready.

Ask around your office to see if anyone has a preview party planned today or tomorrow. If so, ask if you can join them.

If you can't find anyone to tag along with (and don't be surprised if you can't; many agents rarely preview—don't ask me how they keep up on the market), ask your broker if he or she will take you out for an hour. For your very first previewing trip, I highly recommend that you accompany someone else to see how it's done. And remember, you're "invading" someone's home, unlocking their door, looking into their personal things and it's your responsibility to make sure the home is secure when you leave. For your first trip out, let someone else take that responsibility.

How to Preview

Take the MLS printout with you while you're previewing so you can start to associate all the features and abbreviations on the sheet with the actual house you're looking at. Notice how the listing agent describes the features and the condition. Did she exaggerate or euphemize (e.g., "cozy" instead of "claustrophobic")? Did she capture the essence of the home or is her description dull and uninspiring? Did she highlight the best features (in your opinion) or simply run through the list of amenities ("3 bedroom, 2 bath tri-level home in Woodbridge" versus "Dynamite Tri-level Home with Flair!")?

It may be hard to do at this stage, but ask yourself, "Would I pay this price for this home?" As your showing tour progresses, you'll start to form opinions about market value, even on this first day!

JENNIFER'S $0.02...

If you don't seem to be forming such opinions, you might be in the wrong market for your interests. My first office was in the foothills outside of Denver, which was a market that didn't interest me much. I found that on my previewing tours, I had trouble forming opinions about the homes I looked at—they all looked pretty much the same to me, even if the price differential was half a million dollars or more! I had a hard time drawing conclusions about market value or special features, even after several months. I left this office within the year in search of a market that was more in tune with my interests.

Pay attention to how your preview mentor opens the lockbox, greets the seller (if she's home), where he leaves his business card, how much time he spends looking at the home and what he seems to be "looking for." Ask him his opinion of the price.

After you've previewed with another agent or your broker, you'll be able to do it on your own. But before calling to set your first solo previews, ask your broker or office manager for help here also. You'll need to know several things (it's not as simple as it looks!), such as which phone number on the listing sheet to call, your office ID (if applicable), the typical showing windows and advance notice required in your area (e.g., from 2 p.m. to 3 p.m. today), lockbox / key pick-up protocol, etc., etc., etc.

Once you done it the first time, it will be a piece of cake forever. Here's how it's done in my market: "I'm calling to set a preview on 248 Prince Way. My name is Jennifer Allan, with Sell with Soul Real Estate. My office ID is 09182. I'd like to preview the home between 2:00 and 4:00 today." The receptionist or showing service takes my information, calls the seller to schedule the preview and calls my office back with the lockbox combination and any special instructions.

After you've called in your previews, write down the showing information (lockbox, showing window, etc.) on each individual MLS printout. Put the printouts in the order that you're going to look at the homes.

Go look at houses! Don't be early. If you've ever had your own home on the market, you know how annoying that can be. If your showing window is between 11:00 a.m. and noon, don't show up at 10:50. And of course, try to be in and out before noon.

When previewing, try to take in the house as a whole. How does it feel? How does it smell? Does it make you want to move in, or get out? How does it compare to the other homes you've previewed?

Then get specific...how is the floor plan? Flowing or awkward? Does the yard offer privacy or are the neighbors watching your every move? How's the street? The kitchen?

As you're previewing, try not to disturb anything. If you open a closet door, close it. If you use the toilet (don't worry, everyone does it), make sure the lid is exactly how you found it. Sellers really don't want to know that a stranger used their facilities, so don't make it obvious.

Don't worry too much about remembering all the information you're taking in. The goal is not to memorize every single listing in your market; rather it is to practice forming (valid) opinions quickly. Soon, you'll be able to glance at an MLS sheet, breeze through a home in two minutes flat and have a reaction as to whether or not the home is priced fairly. It will happen naturally, I promise you. However, you will need to remember enough about the homes to provide helpful feedback to the listing agents who will be calling you for your comments over the next few days. They are all hoping you have a hot buyer ready to make an offer and might be a little dismayed if you tell them you're just previewing to further your real estate education. In fact, I've been scolded by jerky real estate agents for "wasting" their seller's time previewing for my own benefit.

I once got a listing agent in trouble by previewing for an upcoming open house (more

> Once I previewed a home and attempted to turn on the overhead light using a switch near the front door. Nothing happened. No big deal. Well, the seller called me later that day, furious that I'd touched his light switch. Huh? Turns out that his VCR was plugged into the switched outlet and when I flipped the switch, I turned off his VCR that was programmed to record a show. Now who plugs his VCR into a switched outlet? Sheesh.

on that in a bit). When asked for feedback, I told the listing agent why I was previewing, which he innocently passed on to his seller. The seller (apparently) was furious and fired the listing agent for allowing previews!

So that's previewing. You'll be doing a lot of it in the next few months...and years.

In Case You're Wondering...

In case you're wondering, I do realize that your broker has his or her own training program for you, which may be significantly different from my plan. Moreover, your broker or mentor will have his or her own ideas as to how to best run, promote and expand your business. This shouldn't be a problem. Success in real estate is not dependent on one formula or "program," so feel free to coordinate my ideas with the ideas presented by your broker or mentor. As long as you are working your business, not procrastinating (too much) and showing up every day, you're well on your way to success in your new career.

Chapter Five

Who Knows You?

GENERATING BUSINESS AND REFERRALS FROM THE VERY IMPORTANT PEOPLE WHO KNOW YOU

Excerpted from The Seduction of Your SOI, by Jennifer Allan

"Welcome aboard. Here's your desk, here's your phone. Good luck to you."

Are you ready...to cold call, to knock on doors, to hassle FSBO's and expired listings? Are you excited to hear "no" about 99 times...on your way to one golden "yes"?

No?

(Don't worry, I won't tell your broker. Your secret is safe with me.)

If you shudder at the thought of chasing down your prey, I have great news for you. You don't have to! There is a whole community of people out there, ready and willing to help you jump-start your business. They're known as your Sphere of Influence ("SOI"), a term that by now you're all familiar with, and they include your friends, your family, your acquaintances, your friends' friends, your friends' families, your family's friends and your family's families. Every living, breathing person you know (or will know) has the potential to become your biggest cheerleader and to bring business your way without you even asking for it.

Sound good? It gets better.

SOI business is fun, even for introverts. Depending on your personal preferences, a good SOI business model includes lunch dates, housewarming parties, afternoon BBQ's, friendly e-mail exchanges, cocktails and football games. Conversely, mass-marketing to strangers involves stuffing envelopes, paying for postcards, licking stamps, disturbing day-sleepers, shaking off rejection and designing newspaper ads.

SOI business is relatively cheap. Getting your SOI campaign up and running will cost you a few dollars, but nothing compared to what you'll spend promoting yourself to strangers. You'll likely spend some money on greeting cards, stationery and postage, and you might consider subscribing to a program to create custom emails or eNewsletters. You'll probably need to purchase a real estate-specific contact management system like Top Producer, REST or MoreSolds.

But otherwise, all the money you spend "prospecting" to your SOI will be used getting to know your friends better! Hot wings and beer on Sunday afternoon! All-you-can-eat jumbo shrimp at your house on Friday night! Sushi and sake after work with your best friend on Wednesday!

An SOI business model encourages good habits that stay with you throughout your real estate career. When you commit to developing and maintaining a contact database, you're always aware of the new people you meet. You remember to ask for and write down their contact information and then input it into your management system. Because the success of your business depends on keeping your SOI current, you are more vigilant with updates (even if you aren't perfect).

You won't forget about the nice lady you met last week at your friend's pool party who said she'd like to talk to you about buying an investment property. You can even find her phone number!

An SOI business model minimizes rejection. I don't think anyone, even the most outgoing, charismatic sales dynamo, enjoys rejection. Sure, maybe you can develop a knack for shaking it off, but rejection hurts, even if only for a moment. When you market yourself to strangers, you encounter rejection all the time. Even if it's nothing more than a lackluster response to your expensive advertising, it's disappointing and discouraging.

When your clients are mostly people who know you, or who were referred to you, you are rarely rejected. You may not get every piece of business that crosses your path, but when you don't, it's not from a lack of salesmanship.

An SOI business model increases your accountability. When you are working with friends or referrals, you want to do a GREAT job! Contrary to what some might believe, you won't let things slide just because you have a personal relationship with a client. You want to impress them and even show off a little. This is good. When you do an exceptional job for one client, you raise your own bar a little and feel the need to do as good a job for the next... and even better for the next. Before you know it, you're an extraordinary real estate agent!

Business generated from your SOI is easy business to get. If your friends and your friends' friends think you're a competent real estate agent (or even just a generally competent person) "interviews" will be a slam dunk. You'll rarely have to compete for listings and buyers; they're already predisposed to hire you.

Business generated by your SOI tends to be better business. Assuming the people you know are people you respect and would like to do business with, the business generated by them will also be business you'll enjoy. On the other hand, people who wander into a real estate office or visit an open house or answer a newspaper ad may not be as qualified, motivated or as loyal as you would like. Agents who depend on such marketing venues often find themselves working with buyers and sellers who either aren't ready to move or are working with several different agents around town.

Once your SOI is "built," you can coast through the rest of your real estate career. Sure, your SOI list will need ongoing maintenance, but you'll never have to do another day of prospecting. If you spend your first four years building a truly great SOI, it will take care of you the rest of your days. Over the past five years of my career, I relied solely on business generated by my SOI. Thus, my personal promotion expenses were next to nothing and all my working hours were devoted to my (many) clients. I have been able to make a six-figure income working less than 30 hours a week. That is a beautiful thing.

You can depend on your SOI for 100% of your wildly successful real estate business if you like—without making one cold call. I promise. I'll show you how.

"Fishing from the Friendly Pond"

On my first day as a licensed sales associate, I went to a motivational seminar with my new broker. I don't remember what the seminar was about, but one particular point made by the speaker, Larry Kendall of The Group, Inc., has stuck with me all these years. He called it Fishing from the Friendly Pond. It goes something like this:

When business is a little slow and real estate agents get hungry, they automatically want to ratchet up their advertising. They run newspaper ads, consider advertising on bus benches, do a mailing. They go "Fishing in the Unfriendly Pond" (i.e., strangers). Maybe the additional advertising will work, but more likely it will just be an expense to write off at tax time.

What agents should do (all the time, not just when it's slow) is "Fish from the Friendly Pond." Your friends, your family, your past clients. They care about you (at least more than strangers do) and are much more likely to try to help. Do you know 50 people? No? 25? Sure you do. If 25 people tell 5 friends about you, that's 150 people (your 25 friends + their 125 friends) who know you're in real estate. If those 125 friends of friends mention your name just once, you have 125 more potential clients. So, we're up to 275 people working on your behalf.

That's the Friendly Pond theory. Direct your prospecting efforts toward the people who care about you, not people who have never heard of you.

That sounded good to me. Better than cold calling, anyway.

So, from Day One, I focused all my energy on my fledgling sphere of influence. Did it work? Oh, yeah, it worked. And it can work for you.

♪Make New Friends... But Keep the Old

There are two general, overall activities in a good SOI business plan. The first is to nurture the relationships you already have. The second is to expand your SOI on a daily basis, that is, meet new people.

Nurturing your existing relationships does not mean that you suddenly implement a system to cold call all your friends and announce that you LOVE referrals. Egads! Do this, and you'll quickly find your calls avoided. This is bad for business, not to mention your social life!

No, you nurture your relationships by being a generally nice person who is dependable, reliable, fun to be around...and who happens to be a real estate agent. I have written extensively on this topic; for more information, visit my website at www.SellwithSoul.com or do an online search for Jennifer Allan and SOI.

To expand the membership of your sphere of influence, you must meet new people. Extroverts do this naturally; however, they aren't always adept at gathering contact data from the people they meet. We introverts don't usually relish the idea of social networking, but we tend to be exceptionally diligent about keeping track of those we meet!

"THERE'S NOTHING WRONG WITH MY COMFORT ZONE!"
by Susan Haughton

During my 2nd year in real estate, I was sitting in a training class when my managing broker asked me how many hours a week I prospect. Because I was "rookie of the year" for my office the year prior, he was hoping for something inspirational, I suppose, for the new folks who were in attendance.

I have to give him credit, his jaw didn't drop (although he did seem to cringe ever so slightly) when I said, "None. I don't prospect. I don't ask for referrals. I just have fun with it."

I went on to say if I had to pick up the phone, cold call or knock on doors, I would find another career. I HATE it, absolutely loathe it.

So why do it? I didn't get into real estate to make myself miserable. My primary motivation for getting into real estate, I admit, was to avoid a daily commute and not have to get up in the morning. Seriously.

I have done the "self-sacrificing" thing and I'm done with that. I like being comfortable, I like doing what I like to do...always have. And now, I have a thriving career that is fun and profitable—and it's based on having fun. Not that I don't work hard for my clients—don't get me wrong, I am a total Type A workaholic—but as far as getting new business goes, why schlep around town knocking on doors when I can take friends to lunch, to a concert or invite them to spend a week at our beach house? Why spend $$$ on mail when I can get a tax write-off for taking someone to dinner or for throwing a party at my house?

Step outside the comfort zone? WHY? I like being comfortable!

Four Easy Strategies for Building Your SOI

1. Take Your Friends to Lunch

During my first year, I took my friends to lunch. Simple enough. Friendly lunches, not trying to sell myself or anything like that. And, I swear, I got a client and usually a closing from every single lunch.

I didn't pay for all the lunches myself. I'd treat the first time, she'd pick up the tab the second time. We split it sometimes. It didn't matter, because I wasn't going to lunch to prospect to my friends or to tell them how awesome I was. In fact, I didn't go to lunch with any agenda other than to nurture a relationship I already had. It wasn't a business lunch, it was simply an opportunity to have fun with someone whose company I enjoyed and who thought I was pretty cool too.

When I say I didn't prospect to my friends, that's absolutely true. Frankly, I didn't have that much to say, after all, I was new in the business. I didn't have any great successes to brag about, nor did I have any special programs or packages to promote. The only time my new career came up was when I had a particularly interesting "horror" story to tell about one of my deals; in fact, my friends from these early lunch dates still remember the funny stories from my first year.

So what should you talk about at lunch? You can talk about whatever you want, as long as it's not an infomercial for your real estate business. But obviously, in the course of a social encounter, you will likely talk about your work. Talk about how busy you are but how much fun you are having, even how it's harder than you thought it would be if that's the case. Share your stupid embarrassing mistakes. Stuff like that is memorable! Don't worry; it won't reduce your credibility in your friend's eyes as long as you can laugh at yourself.

After my first year, I was too busy for my take-a-friend-to-lunch campaign. Sure, being busy is a good thing, but it was a mistake on my part to abandon this incredibly successful prospecting tool. Don't make the same mistake.

I saw the magic in action from the other side recently. I purchased a second home in Alabama and my real estate agent took me to lunch to thank me for my business. During our conversation, she mentioned a great little house she'd recently shown that she was considering buying as an investment. My ears perked up and I said I might be interested if she wasn't. She showed me the house the next day and I bought it, as well as another one right down the street. So, just for taking me to lunch ($11.48), my agent made nearly $10,000 in commissions! Well, not quite—I got a 25% referral fee from her for both homes because I'm in the business—very cool. Anyway, you never know who among your friends has money to spend on real estate and/or knows someone who does.

I found that the majority of my early business (over 50%) stemmed from just one spur-of-the-moment lunch date I had my first year. I met David (an agent from Aspen) at a continuing education class and we went to lunch during the break. He referred me to Brian, who was looking for investment properties in Denver. Brian referred me to Steve, who was selling his house next door to Brian and was also an investor. While listing one of Brian's fix-n-flip townhouses, I met Chris, who was looking for fix-n-flip properties and was a custom home builder. While showing Steve a duplex downtown, I met Deborah, the seller of the duplex, who was an out-of-state real estate agent looking for someone to refer business to in Denver. Deborah referred me to Samuel, who referred me to Ken, who referred me to...you get the point.

Just from that one lunch with David from Aspen in 1996, I made over $150,000.

Brian	12 Sales	$43,000
Steve	8 Sales	$28,800
Chris	7 Sales	$30,240
Deborah	5 Sales	$21,600
Deborah's referrals	10 Sales	$43,200

Put this book down and go schedule three lunch dates! Right now.

2. Get Out of the Office

I am a homebody. Someone once called me a high functioning hermit. If I could sell real estate and never leave the house, I'd be one happy woman. But, alas, prospects and future paychecks did not come knocking at my door.

Go do something where you will bump into other people. Just be out there in the world, with your antennae up. Do you have a friend who works at or, better yet, manages a restaurant? Drop by for a salad. Or take your dog to a dog park. If you're single, think of all the hot spots for meeting other singles; they might work for meeting future clients too. Drop in on your favorite mortgage broker just to say hi.

Go ahead and "waste" your time with low-potential prospects. If you get a floor call at the office from a buyer who already has an agent, but can't track him or her down, go ahead and show the house he called on. It won't hurt you and you never know what might come of it. That person might end up being your biggest referral source or even the love of your life!

You'll have no problem finding an audience for your market expertise and professional opinions. Baseball games, concerts in the park, barbecues, weddings—anywhere people congregate and converse with others—are great places to casually start up a conversation about real estate.

Excerpted with permission from
Your Successful Real Estate Career, By Ken Edwards [2]

It is absolutely incredible how widespread the interest in real estate is. Let me illustrate. A year or so ago, I attended a small social gathering at a local restaurant. There were twelve people sitting around the table. After dinner, the word somehow got out that I was in real estate. From that point on, real estate dominated the conversation. One woman, who was a widow, asked me how she should go about finding out how much her home was worth in the event she decided to sell it. Her husband had handled those things. Another woman had a current listing in Arkansas and needed guidance on how that transaction was progressing so she would be able to buy a home locally. A third wanted to know the difference between a mortgage broker and a regular lender, since she was in the process of determining how much home she could afford. When word gets out that you're in real estate, get ready to rock.

3. My Low Tech PDA

In my first year, I had a little system that worked surprisingly well for me. Index cards. I carried around a stack of cards, wrapped in a rubber band. Whenever I talked to someone about real estate, I wrote down his or her name and contact

---

2   Kenneth Edwards, Your Successful Real Estate Career,
     AMACOM, 2007, page 201

information on one side, and on the other, his real estate need or interest. Pretty simple.

It sounds so simple and low-tech, but it works! Sure, you can track your prospects on your computer, but...there is a real difference in taking the time to write down someone's name and real estate need on individual index cards, hold them in your hands and flip through them one by one. It's a very different feeling and a much more powerful way to remind yourself of your prospects.

I'd go through the cards every few days and follow up with the prospects as appropriate. I was always surprised at how quickly I'd forget about these prospects and realized that without the cards, many, many potential clients would have been lost forever. I stopped using the cards at some point and I sometimes wonder how many dozens of sales I missed because I inadvertently blew someone off.

Maybe $100,000 worth? Easily.

4. Be the First One to Call Back

Once you have a little momentum, your phone will start to ring. The first agent to call back and act as if they want the buyer's or seller's business will get the buyer's or seller's business. In my first year, this was a huge factor in my success. I was always the first agent to call back and was always cheerfully ready and willing to show the buyer whatever he or she wanted to see. Did I waste a lot of time with lookie-loo's? Sure. But did I sell more houses than the other rookies in my company? Yep.

I am just as responsive with e-mail, even more so. Internet-savvy buyers (and most are these days) aren't patient sorts. If they e-mail you with an inquiry, they'd really like an answer before they log off the computer for lunch. Sooner, if possible. Many times these prospects will vanish into cyberspace, but really, how much time does it take to acknowledge and respond to an e-mail? Maybe 45 seconds? If you send them some listings, maybe 15 minutes?

So my point is—you have a great chance at snagging some good clients if you seem eager to help them. If you're the first one to respond, either by phone or e-mail, with some enthusiasm in your voice, you're already miles ahead of your competition.

What Didn't Work for Me

Because I was so enthusiastic about my new career, I tried it all. And wasted an incredible amount of money. To drum up business, I did a lot of mailers, from boilerplate newsletters to "Spring Forward" postcards to Just Listed/Just Sold announcements. I think I got one new client in ten years from all my mailings, and that was someone I went to high school with who recognized my name from a Bronco's football schedule I sent out.

I also prospected expired listings with a custom postcard campaign I designed myself and was pretty proud of—and I got one listing that expired again because the seller simply wasn't motivated.

One year I spent $20,000 on newspaper ads that resulted in—zero phone calls. Zero! Once I spent $1,000 on a catered broker luncheon for a $500,000 listing and only 15 agents showed up. I spent one Saturday evening sticking open house flyers under the windshield wipers of cars parked at a church and no one came to the open house anyway.

Let's see, what else? I advertised on bus benches, created beautiful custom magnets, sent out annual calendars and Christmas cards, even offered a lottery for a "Free Listing" one year. None of these efforts were noticeably effective. Getting your name and business card Out There In The World is important, but in the beginning, you really shouldn't be spending your precious marketing dollars this way. I know you feel helpless at times and just want to be doing something productive—so go preview, take a friend to lunch, go to the dog park.

Truthfully, I built my SOI business on four simple techniques. Taking my friends to lunch (huge), getting out in the world with my antennae up, following up on my index cards and being the first to call back. I also held open houses, sat on floor time and did a little farming, but I don't have any great success stories to share with you from those activities. I remember being bored and discouraged though, which is the last thing you need while you're trying to build momentum.

JENNIFER'S BLOG
Selling Real Estate Is Not a Numbers Game

You've heard the cold caller's philosophy...for every 100 phone calls you make, you'll get five appointments; for every five appointments you go on, you'll get one listing. Therefore, if you make 500 phone calls, you can count on five listings as a result. If your average listing commission is $5,000, then every phone call is worth $50 since it takes 100 phone calls to get a listing. Supposedly, you will actually start to enjoy hearing "no," because you realize that after 99, you'll hear a "yes," which leads to a paycheck. Every "no" means you are one step closer to a "yes"—sound fun?

Not to me. In fact, it sounds like an awful way to make a living—pestering people for three hours a day. Asking the poor sap who answers the phone if he "knows anyone who's thinking of buying or selling real estate." Being rejected 99 times out of a hundred, voluntarily? Icky. Phooey. Blech.

So, tell us how you really feel, Jennifer!

Okay, thanks, I will.

The State of Colorado's Division of Real Estate did not grant me a real estate license so I could be a professional prospector. I have to assume they intended for me to spend a significant amount of my time serving the clients I am honored to have today instead of tracking down the ones I hope to have tomorrow. Taking good care of my listings and my buyers is my first priority, not an afterthought when I can squeeze them in around my prospecting and networking efforts.

But, but, but...!

Yeah, I know. As self-employed types, we have to ensure ourselves a steady stream of business to keep the home fires burning in the style to which we intend to become accustomed. Hey, believe me, I never took a vow of poverty and I don't sell real estate out of the goodness of my heart. I've had $50,000 months before, more than once, and I could happily get used to that!

But you know what? I have never cold called; I have never knocked on a stranger's door.

For ten years I depended on my SOI for 100% of my business and they generously delivered. Sure, I picked up the odd client here and there from floor time or open houses; maybe two or three a year, which is nothing to sneeze at, but the vast majority of my business comes directly or indirectly from the people I know or meet.

Every client is special to me—even precious. Okay, admittedly some are a pain in the butt, but I still appreciate their business and the juicy commission checks I get as a reward for putting up with them. But most of my clients are pleasant people with real estate needs who simply want to be treated as if their business is valuable to me. Not like a number.

When you depend on your SOI for business, you bow out of the numbers game and it's wonderful. No more dragging yourself to the phone for your daily cold calling session. No more searching the real estate ads for your next FSBO target. No more beating yourself up because you'd rather take a nap than finish up your ten HouseValues CMAs that are due today.

When your pipeline is running low, have a little Super Bowl party or send out some friendly personal e-mails or ratchet up your "take-a-friend-to-lunch" campaign. You don't need 20 more clients today; just two or three good ones will restore your mood and pad your bank account.

SOI business is good business. It's loyal business. It's fun business. The success ratios are more like 50% to 75%, compared to 5% to 10% from traditional lead generation (and that's being optimistic!). So, 100 leads from your SOI will result in 50-75 closings from you.

So how does it work exactly? Glad you asked.

SOI business comes in one lead at a time. But the leads are good leads, leads that will likely result in a closing. Depending on your market and your broker split, each lead-that-will-probably-result-in-a-closing is worth thousands of dollars to you.

So let's say you have a cheering section of 20 friends. If you have implemented a respectful, consistent SOI campaign, you will be the agent of choice for most of them if any happen to need a real estate agent this year. Maybe that will only get you one or two sales; or maybe, if your friends are a restless bunch, you'll get five or six.

You should also get the family business of your 20 nearest and dearest. Katie's grandma moves to town to be closer to her grandchildren. Fred's brother-in-law needs a referral to a Las Vegas agent. Maria's sister gets engaged and needs to sell her condo. Her fiancé wants to sell his too. There's a good chance you'll get first dibs on this sort of business. So let's say you pick up three family members.

Let's not forget everyone else your 20 friends know. If just half of your friends refer you to just one person, that's 10 more clients for you. What if all of your friends refer you to one other person or if three of your friends each refer you to five of their friends? What if you have 30 friends? 50?

Oh, and what about everyone else in your SOI? The other 150 people you know and stay in touch with — your husband's assistant, your dog trainer, your massage therapist? Depending on the strength of your SOI campaign, you might see 5-15 sales a year from these folks.

We haven't even talked about the NEW friends you're going to make over the next 12 months! If you're out there in the world, with your antenna up, you will run into people who happen to be in need of real estate services. If you approach them correctly, that business is yours. That may result in another five sales for you.

So add it all up and you're selling some real estate! All without treating anyone like a number.

Unless you're striving to be a mega-producer with ten buyer agents scurrying around underfoot, you really don't need to go after every buyer and seller in town. This is what I mean when I say real estate is not a numbers game. The business you can generate from your SOI and from your own social encounters really ought to be enough.

■ ■ ■ ■ ■

mastering your domain

LEARNING YOUR PRODUCT...
AND YOUR PRODUCT IS PROPERTY

One of your major projects as a rookie real estate agent is to learn your market. Market expertise is by far the best way to build credibility and jump start your career. Although building market expertise is labor-intensive, I think you'll enjoy it, because it means looking at houses! It may take years for you to become the expert on every neighborhood in your city, if ever. But you gotta start somewhere, right?

A few years ago I considered moving to Florida. Tired of the Colorado snow, I made an exploratory trip with the goal to see if Florida felt like "home" and, if so, could I afford to live on or near the beach?

JENNIFER'S $0.02...

It's a good reality check for you, as a real estate agent, to see what it feels like on the other side. You will be reminded how vulnerable and dependent on you your clients are, especially when they are new to your area.

I had never shopped for real estate in Florida and had no familiarity with the market. I walked into a real estate office in Ft. Lauderdale and asked for the agent on floor duty. Judy Johnson offered to help me. I told her my story and gave her my general price range. I told her I wanted to live near the beach, hoping she wouldn't laugh at me (I didn't know the market, maybe I was asking for the impossible). She didn't laugh, which was encouraging—she just said, "Well, let's just go over to the computer and see what's available."

Judy struggled a bit with the computer. She couldn't seem to get the MLS system to load, and when it did, she had trouble identifying which MLS areas near the beach fell into my price range. She did her first search, which turned up nothing. She said, "Oops, I accidentally asked for co-ops, not condos." She ran her search again, and turned up eight properties. She couldn't figure out how to access the additional pictures of these eight properties.

As it turned out, none of the properties were that close to the beach anyway, and most were age-restricted—i.e., the buyer had to be at least 55 years old.

After almost two hours of this, she printed out listings for several condos and houses (don't ask about the struggle with the printer), gave me a map and asked me to drive by the homes. I was worn out, hungry and much less enthusiastic than I had been two hours ago. I headed out, map and listings in hand, fully intending to do my drive-by's. Instead I ended up stopping at Denny's for lunch and driving back to my hotel for a nap, frustrated and unhappy with Ft. Lauderdale.

Two days later, I wandered across Alligator Alley and found myself in Naples, Florida. I walked into a Re/Max office and talked to the agent on floor duty, Jim Peterson. I told Jim my story and this was his response:

"Well, Jennifer, if you want to live right on the beach, you'll definitely be looking at a high-rise condo. Prices for beach-front two-bedroom condos start around $400,000. Your monthly HOA dues will run anywhere from $300/month to $600/month. Some allow pets, but most don't. Now, if you're willing to live three blocks from the beach, we can find you a town-home for around $300,000. If you really want a house, we can get you within two miles of the beach, but anything closer will be over a million. Let me show you some of my favorite projects and see what you think."

Whew, didn't that feel better? Don't you think I felt much better cared for? Doesn't this agent sound like the one who can make my dreams of beachfront living come true? Or not, as it turned out, since my dream of a beachy home was out of my price range. But wasn't it better to know that in five minutes rather than two hours?

Jim was just doing his job. Our job as real estate agents is to know the market (and our systems!) better than our customers. We are well paid for our knowledge as well as our ability to share that knowledge with our customers. In this age of technology, anyone can pull up information on the properties for sale; it's our job to efficiently match that data with the person sitting in front of us.

Your product is property. Whatever your specialty is—single family homes, condos, vacation rentals, vacant land, new homes, old homes, ugly homes— you should know more than your audience about your product. As a newer agent, you can't call on experience you don't yet have; your experience level is beyond your immediate control. What you can control is your knowledge of your market.

JENNIFER'S BLOG
Why She Lost the $700,000 Buyer...

Her heart is broken. She feels rejected. She wants to hang up her real estate license and crawl under a rock.

Why? Because her $700,000 buyer prospect chose another agent.

She's beating herself up. She's asking herself, "Did I not dress the part?" "Was my car not nice enough?" She wonders if she should have worn her fancy leather boots and more make-up (she lives in Texas, after all). Maybe she should have borrowed her sister's Mercedes SUV.

No, no, I assure her. It's not your dress or your car. It's actually worse than that. Worse, as in, it's going to be a little tougher for you to swallow.

I'll bet 100 pennies that the Other Agent knew the market better than my broken-hearted friend. I'll bet that when the Buyer met with this Other Agent, the Other Agent was able to speak intelligently about the $700,000 market and even mention a few of the listings she was familiar with. I bet she got the Buyer all revved up and excited. I bet she said, "Oh, you must see this new listing that just came on the market yesterday! It has two master suites, both with Jacuzzi tubs, a beautiful view and the most amazing gourmet kitchen!" She probably then clinched it with, "Are you free on Saturday? Around 10?"

Now that, my friend, is how you capture a $700,000 Buyer. By knowing the market and speaking intelligently about it. When you know the market, confidence oozes from you. And confidence draws buyers to agents like bees to honey.

And of course, she closed the deal by making an appointment. As soon as possible.

But here's the good news. For my friend. Before discovering that the $700,000 Buyer had ditched her, she previewed, previewed, previewed. She now knows an awful lot about the upper-end market in her Texas town. The next time a high-dollar prospect knocks on her door, the conversation will go much differently. My friend will know how many bedrooms and baths $700,000 gets you. How many acres and how many garage spaces. She'll know. She'll speak with confidence. She'll make the appointment. She'll get the buyer.

When you're new in real estate, you can't know the nuances of every neighborhood, of every price range. That takes time and experience. But you can hurry up the process with aggressive previewing. As your career matures, you will be familiar with more and more neighborhoods. You'll speak more intelligently about them, more of the time. Your buyer closing ratio will improve every year. It's something to look forward to...!

THREE WAYS TO LEARN YOUR MARKET FAST

1. Preview with a Purpose

The best way I know of to increase your product knowledge is to preview. Previewing means scheduling appointments to look at listed properties without a buyer. Get out there and start looking at homes! But, if you're like me, previewing without a real purpose is a waste of time. I need a reason to preview that makes the information I glean "stick" with me.

So, come up with a purpose for your previewing. One great way is to preview around an open house you're doing next Sunday. Since you may not have any listings of your own yet, offer to do open houses for other agents (we'll talk about this more in Chapter Seven). Go look at the house you are holding open and then schedule previews of the other homes for sale in the immediate neighborhood.

I call this "Opinionated Previewing" because it's much easier to evaluate and absorb the appeal and features of a home if you have something to compare it to. Pretend you are working with a buyer who is looking for something similar to the home you are holding open (if all goes well at your open house, you may be!). At each home, ask yourself if it is a home you would show a prospective buyer. Look with a critical eye—does it show well? Does it seem to be priced appropriately? If it needs work, is there room in the market for an investor to make a little money? Does the home "wow" you when you walk in the door?

Have I lost you? Are you asking yourself, what's the point of all this previewing? Wasn't this chapter supposed to be about learning your market, not preparing for your open house?

Yes, and let me get back to topic. Every single time you preview with a purpose, I can almost guarantee you a sale or a listing. It's that powerful. I can't tell you how many times I previewed homes for one reason or another and that very night met someone who lived in the same building as a condo I looked at, or next door to a home I toured. Do you think you sound like a brand new agent when you can casually say to someone you just met, "Oh, there's a unit in your building for sale, isn't there? What a great location, right across from the park! What's going on with the construction next door?"

You don't have to tell them you were out previewing just that day. No! You act as if you know every property in town because, after all, you are a professional real estate agent who keeps up on the market. Talk about building credibility! Real estate is almost always a hot topic in a social setting and if you sound as if you know your stuff, you'll hand out lots of business cards.

The trick is sounding as if you are the local expert. There's always someone in a roomful of people who is thinking about moving or buying an investment property, and the more you know about the market, the easier it is to catch his or her attention. When you speak with confidence about the real estate market, people listen.

Sure, when you're a rookie, you don't know the nuances of every neighborhood, condominium project or new subdivision. This will come with time. But the more you're out there, the quicker you'll be the expert. And it's great fun to be a Jim Peterson, the savvy agent from Florida!

2. Do Five Practice CMA's

Another great way to learn your market fast is doing a CMA. "CMA" is industry jargon for a Comparative Market Analysis (or some call it a Competitive Market Analysis). It's simply a report prepared by a real estate agent to determine the approximate market value of a home. The CMA is usually presented to a seller prospect during a listing appointment (discussed in detail in Chapter Nine).

> **CMA**
>
> *CMA stands for Competitive Market Analysis or Comparative Market Analysis. A CMA is a report prepared by a real estate agent to determine the market value of a home.*

Unless you already have a listing appointment scheduled, you'll have to come up with your own properties to price for your five CMA's.

Here are some ideas:

Your Own Home

If you live in a residential property (that is, a property that can be bought or sold rather than an apartment or a tent), you can easily prepare a CMA for your home. The steps involved in pricing a home are:

> 1. Pull up the county tax record for the home. Hopefully it is available online; if not, I'd move to a different market. Just kidding, sort of. You're looking for square footage, age of home, lot size, etc.

> 2. Drive by the home (if it's yours, you can skip this step!).

> 3. Search the MLS for market information, specifically: Recent Comparable Sales and Currently Active Listings. Use the search tips discussed in Chapter Nine.

> 4. Preview the Currently Active Listings.

> 5. Drive by the Recent Comparable Sales.

> 6. Review your data and determine the market value range.

Again, Chapter Nine discusses each of these steps in detail.

Your Friends' Homes

Think of two people who know you're brand new and you feel comfortable telling you'd like to use them as guinea pigs. Ask if you can come by sometime soon to see their home. Even if you're familiar with their home, you'll need to go see it again, looking at it through the eyes of a real estate agent. It's good practice and you will see a lot of things you never noticed before.

When you meet with your friends at their homes, dress nicely; after all, you are trying to make a good impression on them. If you want your friend to refer you to his friends, he needs to see you as someone professional and presentable. Depending on your history with him, you might have a little work to do here!

Take notes as you walk through the home with your friend, ask intelligent questions ("Do you know how old the furnace is? The roof? Have you made any significant improvements to the home since you purchased it? Do you feel you paid a fair price for the home?"). Of course, he isn't planning to sell his home right now, but people like to talk about their homes and you'll sound as if you know what you're doing.

I can't stress enough how your friendly professionalism will earn you big bonus points with your best friends. If they believe in you, they will be your biggest referral sources. But just because you've been friends since birth doesn't mean they automatically have faith that you're a great real estate agent. You'll have to earn that. It's well worth the effort.

After meeting with your friend at his house, start working on the CMA right away. Preview the competition, review the recent sales, go ahead and put together a full listing presentation including the CMA and pricing recommendation.

Make an appointment to meet with your friend to present your findings. Ask him to bear with you while you go through the entire presentation. Welcome his feedback. If you hate to role-play (as I do), it might make you feel better to know that your friend is probably truly interested in what you have to say. It's not every day someone takes so much interest in him and his home.

Your Company's Listings

You need to make an effort to see as many of your office listings as you can, because a knowledge of your own company's inventory can help you in several ways. First, if your office offers (or requires) "floor time" (a block of time an agent is required to be at the office to take incoming telephone inquiries or meet with walk-in prospects), you'll need to be familiar with the listings these prospects will be asking about. Second, listing agents will appreciate your interest in their properties and may feed you leads they get from sign calls or Internet inquiries if they're too busy to handle them. And of course, you are building your market knowledge which is critical to your success.

After you've previewed, choose one or two office listings that appeal to you and do your own CMA for them. In other words, pretend you are the listing agent and come up with your opinion of the market value. Go through the entire process – pull up the county tax record, preview the competition and review the sold data. When you've completed your CMA, compare it to the listed price of the property. If your analysis of the right price is significantly different from the actual list price, ask your broker to review your results with you. You might just be right! Pricing a home is an art, not a science and even experienced agents overprice their listings sometimes. And of course, if your analysis is faulty, it will be educational for you to learn where you went wrong.

If you do five of these CMA's, you will have taken a huge step toward being a professional real estate agent. The next time you only have 24 hours to prepare for a listing appointment, you'll be glad you got all this practice!

3. Go House-Hopping with a Friend

Do any of your friends own their home? Offer to take them on a tour of the homes for sale in their neighborhood, just for fun. If you're new and haven't yet worked with many (any?) buyers, you'll get practice selecting properties, setting showings, planning your route, opening lockboxes, and of course, showing houses. You'll also have a buddy to compare homes with and discuss the appeal and features of each. If you're showing homes in your friend's own neighborhood, he will be full of opinions for you!

OTHER LEARNING-YOUR-MARKET IDEAS

- Visit open houses.
- Drive a new way to the office or grocery store.
- Visit neighborhood parks.
- Ask your friends to tell you what they like and dislike about their neighborhoods.
- Play with Zillow.com.
- Read local neighborhood newspapers.
- Preview with other agents if the opportunity arises.
- Subscribe to other agents' newsletters (if they specialize in a particular neighborhood).
- Try out different grocery stores.
- Visit an unfamiliar shopping mall.

Chapter Seven

open sunday!
your first open house

HOLDING OPEN HOUSES FOR OTHERS

At some point early on in your real estate career, you'll be asked about doing an open house for another agent. Why would you do such a thing? Because, open houses are touted as being great places to meet unattached buyers; that is, buyers who don't already have an agent. Typically, when you hold an open house for another agent, any prospects you pick up at the open house are yours to keep, without even paying a referral fee for them.

Why would the listing agent offer this opportunity to you? Doesn't she want to pick up prospects for herself?

Uh, no. Most experienced agents dread holding open houses. The reasons why are many and varied and we don't need to go into them here. At some point in your career, you may dread them too, but for now, it's probably better to allow you to draw your own conclusions!

Anyway, in order to maximize the productivity of your open house, you have some work to do ahead of time.

Let's get started.

Check Out the Competition

Before you attempt to hold your own open house, you should probably spend a Sunday afternoon visiting other open houses. Subtly check out the styles of the agents holding the open houses.

- Do they look enthusiastic when they greet visitors? Or bored? Or scared?

- Do they follow visitors around or do they barely look up from their novel?

- Do they ask guests to sign in?

- Do they attempt to prospect to visitors? If so, at what point? When the visitor walks in the door or as he's leaving?

- Do the agents provide refreshments? Do they display promotional material?

- How about the signage, both directional arrows leading you to the open house and in front of the home?

- Which agents made you feel comfortable in the home and why? Which agents made you feel nervous...and why?

By the way, don't be afraid to tell the agent holding the open house that you're a new agent just checking things out. But whatever you do, DON'T make conversation with other visitors—the agent may interpret this as an attempt to "steal" her buyer prospects!

At the end of the day, put it all together and come up with your own plan for the Perfect Open House...YOUR way!

JENNIFER'S $0.02...

At Your Open House

Before I continue, I must make one point crystal clear. While I know that the primary reason you are holding an open house is to prospect for buyers, please don't ever forget that the reason the seller is allowing you the opportunity to camp out in his home is that he wants you to sell his house. This really is your first responsibility, so don't embarrass yourself or the listing agent by being too obvious about your true intentions. Put yourself in the seller's shoes—he spent all day Saturday dusting, vacuuming, cleaning out closets and pantries and mowing the lawn (hopefully!) to prepare for his open house. He might have even baked cookies or prepared lemonade. He's truly excited about the idea of his home selling today as a result of your efforts!

Prepare for Your Visitors

Okay, to continue with preparing for your open house.

The best way to build rapport with open house visitors is to be familiar not only with the home you're holding open, but also with the other homes in the area. If you sound like the market expert, serious buyers will be drawn to you. So, let's make that happen.

You need preview as much of the competition as you can, prior to your open house. Ideally, you'll have time to preview the direct competition as well as properties priced higher and lower than your open house.

So, as time permits, your priorities in previewing around an open house are as follows:

First, the competing listings
Homes near your open house in the same general price range. It's also a good idea to preview any other homes for sale on the same block, regardless of price.

Second, any lower priced listings
Homes near your open house that are priced lower than your open house.

Third, any higher priced listings
Homes near your open house that are priced higher than your open house.

Fourth, competing listings in comparable neighborhoods
Similarly priced homes in other neighborhoods that are similar in appeal to the neighborhood of your open house.

After you've previewed, identify the ten best listings you saw. Bring printouts of those listings to the open house with you.

The Day of Your Open House

Here is a checklist of everything you'll need to take with you for your first open house.

- The detailed MLS printout of the home you're holding open
- Open house signs
- Balloons and/or flags
- A stack of your business cards
- The home brochures you created for the open house
- Printouts of the listings you previewed with your comments
- Clean printouts of the Top 10 previewed listings printouts (the best listings you found while previewing)
- Notepad & index cards
- A blank purchase contract
- A sign-in sheet and pen (if desired)
- Cookies (if desired) and napkins
- A book and/or laptop computer
- Music
- Toilet paper (if the home is vacant)
- A chair (if the home is vacant)
- Scented candles or fragrance (just in case)

Be on time for your open house. Remember, you are representing the listing agent who is counting on you to make a good impression on his seller. If the seller has to call the listing agent to find out where the heck you are, that's not a good beginning to the afternoon. Allow plenty of time to put up your directional arrows and make sure you place them in highly visible locations.

When you arrive at the home, be prepared for people to come through the door as soon as your Open House sign is up. It always happens that way for some reason—you'll get a flood of visitors right at the beginning when you're setting up and at the end when you're closing down. Anyway, before putting up your sign, go through the home, turn on lights, open curtains, check to make sure everything is clean and tidy.

Display your brochures and business cards, set yourself up somewhere comfortable, but not in the "best" room of the home. If the home has a spectacular living room, don't park yourself in there. You want visitors to explore the home thoroughly and to take note of special features or rooms. If you're in a "special" room, your presence there will distract visitors from it.

A soulful reminder: you are in that home to sell that home; that is your first obligation. Don't make the rookie mistake of trying to talk to visitors about other homes while they're still taking in the details of this one. Imagine that the seller is watching you with a hidden video camera (who knows?). Don't do anything the seller wouldn't approve of. And don't leave early unless the home is vacant. Sellers know exactly what time you leave—either they're parked across the street watching or they have neighbors spying on you. I'm serious.

Everyone develops their own style for holding open houses. You can be assertive...or not so. You can show visitors around...or let them wander. You can require sign in...or not. You can ask a lot of questions...or just wait for the visitors to approach you.

Me? Well, being me, I take the soft sell approach. I do not require sign-in, I do not show visitors around, I ask questions, but only of people who seem open to my advances. If I connect with someone, I am happy to chat with them about the home, or the state of the market. If I do not feel a good connection with a visitor, I just smile and let him approach me if he needs anything.

JENNIFER'S $0.02...

Because I'm an introvert, open houses have been a little nerve-wracking from Day One to Day 4,000...making small talk with strangers for three hours just isn't high on my list of comfortable activities. I found the best way to ease my tension was to have music playing (so that it's not deadly silent when there's only me and one visitor in the house) and to have my laptop computer set up and open on the kitchen table. I could look up from my laptop to greet a new visitor, which gave me something to be doing besides standing there looking anxious.

If your open house is lively, you will have an opportunity to talk about the homes you previewed. When an open house has good energy, people are talking to you and to each other, usually about real estate. It's easy for you to chime in with your two cents or to casually mention the fabulous house around the corner (if appropriate).

When It's Time to Go,
Make Sure You:

- Turn off lights & close curtains (as you found them).
- Clean up any trash left by visitors.
- Close closet doors, shower doors, check toilets.
- Make sure all exterior doors are secure.
- Take your home brochures with you.

Leave a nice note for the seller with some commentary on the open house, including the approximate number of visitors and any feedback.

Take down the Open Sunday rider.

Call the listing agent on your way home to tell him how the open house went and to thank him profusely for allowing you to hold his listing open. If you do a good job for this guy, he can be a gold mine for you. When he's busy, he might just be looking for someone to help him with more open houses, sign calls or other lower priority referrals. If you sense he might be interested, offer to take sign calls for him and to pay him a referral fee for any closings that result from these calls. Many busy agents are happy to refer these types of leads.

That Evening
or The Next Day... at the Latest

Follow up with any buyers you met at the open house. If someone asked you a question you promised to research, do the research right away and call him with the answer. If a potential buyer asked you to e-mail her listings, do it tonight. It's a good idea to call her when you send them, which may solidify the relationship a bit. I actually met my first real estate agent at an open house. She called me that night to follow up and I happily hired her to find me a home. She represented me in the purchase of four houses over the next few years before I got my own license. Remember, if you act as if you want a buyer's business, you will get the buyer's business. Most agents don't follow up promptly (or at all), so if you do, you'll be a step ahead of the competition, even if you're new.

Have fun!

your first buyer

EIGHT STEPS TO FINDING "THE ONE"

Your broker will walk you through the showing protocol of your market area—scheduling showings, showing appointment windows, lockbox and/or key pickup. This part is easy. My goal is to help you with the nuances that they don't teach you in real estate school or office training, and give you some hints so you look as if you've been showing houses to buyers for years.

In general, the home-buying process looks something like this:

1. Pre-qualify the buyer
2. Show properties to the buyer
3. Find "The One" and make a written offer on it
4. Negotiate the offer with the seller's agent
5. If the offer is successfully negotiated, the buyer inspects the home
6. Buyer obtains loan approval
7. Final Walk-thru
8. Closing

Pre-qualifying Buyers

Many real estate instructors make quite a fuss about financially pre-qualifying your buyers. They advise you to either pre-qualify them yourself (I've never done this) or send them off to your lender right away. I more or less agree.

However, remember to treat your new buyer the way you would like to be treated. Imagine how you would feel if, at your first meeting with a real estate agent, he only seemed to care about your financial qualifications and not about your housing needs. When you are working with a brand new buyer, you need to build rapport if you ever want to hear from him or her again. If you immediately shuttle him off to your lender as if you couldn't be bothered even talking with him, you will likely lose that buyer to another, more soulful agent who makes him feel special.

> **LENDER**
> *The person who handles the buyer's loan, also known as a mortgage broker.*

CAUTION!

Beware of writing an offer for a buyer who hasn't yet spoken with a lender; it's not only a waste of time, it's disrespectful to the seller, the listing agent and the entire process.

Besides, it won't hurt you to "waste" your time talking with a buyer who isn't qualified to purchase a home just yet. It won't even hurt you to show her homes once or twice; if nothing else, you'll add a little something to your market knowledge—always a good thing. If she can't buy a house today, she may very well be able to buy in a year (and that year will be here before you know it).

But there's a difference between someone who isn't quite ready to buy and someone who is just using you to entertain her. It's perfectly reasonable for you to ask a new buyer prospect to call a lender so both of you have a solid price range to work with. If the buyer resists you at this point, you can safely assume she isn't serious and will likely vanish on you. A buyer who wants to buy a house is looking to you for guidance on the process. If you tell a real buyer to call a lender, she will happily call a lender.

Showing Houses to Buyers

It looks and sounds a lot easier than it is. I still struggle sometimes picking the right homes to show buyers, especially if I'm working in an unfamiliar neighborhood. If you live in a metropolitan area, it will be years before you know your way around every neighborhood in town, if ever. It's mortifying to get lost while showing houses, and if your buyer is from out of town—in town for the weekend to buy a house—you might even lose her business if you don't appear to know your city.

Find the One, Make an Offer

You will develop your own style for showing homes and I don't think there's one "right" way to do it. Some agents follow their buyers around, pointing out the obvious. "And this is the kitchen!" I let my buyers wander around as they please while I explore the house on my own. It allows them to discover the home for themselves without distracting input from me.

You will also develop a knack for recognizing when buyers want to make an offer on a house—when to push them, when to back off. Many real estate books will give you a variety of closing methods designed to get your buyer to the table writing an offer.

Excerpted from
Your Successful Real Estate Career, by Ken Edwards [3]

[Regarding closing techniques] The most prevalent theory, encountered in almost all sales training programs, is that folks need to be helped along in the decision-making process. To do this, a whole series of closing techniques has been devised, named, catalogued and taught. Each is designed to facilitate the process as you guide your prospects smoothly and efficiently toward the major close by achieving a series of "minor closes" (less important decisions the client makes along the way).

Those who question the appropriateness of procedures such as this do so on the grounds that they are manipulative and hence unprofessional. They maintain that the only acceptable closing technique is to provide people all the information they need to make an informed choice, and then permit them the courtesy of reaching their decision in their own time.

---

3   Kenneth Edwards, Your Successful Real Estate Career,
     AMACOM, 2007, page 101

I tend toward the soft sell, perhaps even softer than I should, because buyers do need to be pushed a little sometimes. They want to buy, but are scared. Or perhaps they are waiting for you to show them what the next step is (it's obvious to you, but not to them).

Your personality and personal style will lead you down the correct path, for you. But at the very least, offer to draft up a contract for their review.

If your buyers think they have found a house they love, but aren't sure, tread carefully. I think the old cliché is true—that they will know it when they see it, and I tell my buyers this. I don't want them to make an offer on a home they don't love because they will probably want out of the deal somewhere down the road. Lots of hassle for me, an inconvenience to the sellers and a real buzz-kill for the buyers. If I sense that my buyers are ambivalent about a home, even if they're ready to make an offer, I'll try to put them off overnight. I don't want them to feel undue pressure from me because it will be All My Fault when they can't sleep a few nights later, wracked with buyer's remorse.

Some buyers simply aren't emotional, but this is the exception, not the norm. Even professional investors get a little excited when you find them a good deal. Buyers who aren't excited are either worried about something they haven't told you about or aren't emotionally attached to the home. Assure them that they have all the time in the world (as far as you're concerned) and that it may take several trips to find the right house. When they see that you're not pressuring them to make a quick decision, their trust in you will increase dramatically, making your job easier and much more fun.

Preparing the Offer

Explain to your buyer that the offer is a written proposal between the buyer and the seller. The offer outlines the buyer's desired price, financial terms, dates and deadlines, personal property inclusions, and other details. If the seller signs the offer as written, the offer becomes a binding contract. If the seller makes any changes to the offer, in the form of a counterproposal, the seller has technically rejected the offer and the buyer is free to walk away. Either party is free to rescind his offer or counteroffer at any time prior to written acceptance by the other party. (This is how it works in Colorado; your state may have different laws.)

Spend at least an hour going through the purchase contract with your buyer. Explain in detail how the inspection provision works since this is an area of significant concern for buyers. Also ensure that your buyer understands her rights and responsibilities regarding the loan application and approval process.

You'll develop your own "rap" for explaining contracts to buyers, but try to keep in mind that this may be the first time your buyer has ever seen a real estate purchase contract. She may be making assumptions she doesn't know to ask you about. For example, make sure she knows that her earnest money deposit check will be cashed if the offer is accepted. I've found that many buyers think it is held until closing.

The purchase contract is overwhelming and intimidating. Assure your buyer that you will be carefully tracking the deadlines with her, so she need not worry about missing an important date. Later in this chapter, we'll discuss date tracking in more detail.

Everyone Likes to Negotiate...

...regardless of any claim to the contrary. It's tempting to put together a low offer

> **EARNEST MONEY**
> *The deposit check written by the buyer when making an offer on a property. If the offer is successfully negotiated, earnest money is deposited into an escrow account and credited back to the buyer at closing. If the buyer defaults on the contract, the earnest money may be retained by the seller.*
>
> **BUYER AGENT**
> *The real estate agent representing the buyer, usually with a written buyer agency agreement.*

for a buyer and declare to the listing agent that, "This is our final and best offer." But it won't work. The seller doesn't want to accept an offer as written, unless it's full price, and a buyer will actually be dismayed if her first (low) offer is accepted. She'll wonder if she could have/should have offered less.

As a buyer agent, encourage strong offers, but remember that you represent your buyer, not your commission check. If your buyer wants to offer low, even after you've shown her data that indicates the home is priced fairly, go ahead and put the offer together. Don't whine and fuss and, by all means, don't be embarrassed about presenting the offer to the listing agent. Your job is to get your buyer client the best price and if your words or body language indicate to the listing agent that your offer sucks and you know it—you just breached your duty to your buyer.

Besides, you never know what the seller will accept. I've tried to convince my buyers to offer more than they want to (and I usually lose) and lo and behold—the seller accepts their low offer! Talk about losing credibility with my buyers in a single bound. Oops. I'm making light of the situation, but it can get pretty ugly, pretty quickly. If you give your buyer any reason to suspect that you don't have his best interest at heart, you will lose his trust and probably his business.

That said, you can make the choice to let your buyer go if he truly is not motivated. If a buyer is motivated, he will usually abandon the lowball-offer strategy after trying it a few times.

Let's assume you've successfully negotiated your offer and you're now under contract! Yippeeeeeeee!

Start Scheduling Inspections

INSPECTION

This is the contractually agreed upon time period where the buyer has the right to inspect the physical condition of the property. In some regions, this is also understood to include an investigation by the buyer into the crime rates, public school data, demographics or any other non physical "feature" of the property. If the buyer is dissatisfied with the condition of the property, physical or otherwise, he must object before the inspection objection deadline or the seller can assume that the buyer accepts the property "as is."

Don't spend your commission check quite yet. In some markets, inspections can kill a significant number of your sales if you're having a run of bad luck.

Always recommend that your buyer inspect the home to his satisfaction. Most trainers tell you to give your buyers a list of at least three names of general inspectors so that they can choose. Of course, the buyer may hire any inspector he likes outside of your list, or inspect the home himself if that's what he wants. But do advise him to hire a general inspector and encourage him to get any other inspections that are typical in your market.

In Denver, for example, I always recommend a sewer line inspection. If your buyer is concerned about radon, by all means tell him to have it checked out. Don't ever, ever, ever talk your buyer out of an inspection; regardless of your intentions, it will be perceived as an attempt to save your paycheck. And, there might be some truth to that.

Whether or not to attend the inspection is a topic of hot debate. Attorneys will tell you to avoid the physical inspection, or, if you must attend, "stand outside and smoke a cigarette." Their point is that the inspection findings are between the buyer and his inspector and your presence there might somehow make you partially liable for the physical condition of the home.

I found this advice to sound good on paper (or in a GRI class), but impractical in practice. Why?

> 1. It's hard to negotiate repairs found during inspection that you didn't see firsthand.

> 2. Your buyer expects you to be there and your credibility will take a little hit if you don't attend.

> 3. It's good customer service.

> 4. When you're new, inspections are an excellent opportunity to further your real estate education.

> 5. You need to be able to recommend good inspectors to your buyers and if you don't attend inspections, how can you judge?

I don't see any way to avoid attending inspections without sacrificing the quality of your service to your buyer client, even at a risk of taking on the above-mentioned liability. However, of course, I am not an attorney!

A typical inspection will reveal many minor maintenance concerns and often one major concern. A kitchen sink that leaks, a few improperly wired electrical outlets, a missing downspout, a slow-draining bathtub or asbestos-wrapped ductwork are usually easy fixes. Major concerns might be a damaged roof, a broken sewer line, an inoperable or dangerous heating system, structural stress or damage, or an outdated electrical system.

Handled correctly, inspections can almost always be successfully negotiated. Even if your buyer's laundry list of minor items is three pages long and he insists on asking the seller to repair each and every one, you can usually hold this deal together.

Drafting the Inspection Request

The goal is to create a punch list or inspection request list for the seller that doesn't feel abusive or punitive. We want the seller to agree to as many items as possible, without much back and forth negotiation.

Go through the inspection report with your buyer and identify the items he feels strongly about. Group the concerns into categories such as Plumbing, Electrical, HVAC, etc. If there is a major issue (e.g., the roof or furnace needs replacement), this is the first item on your request. Always ask that the major repairs be corrected by a licensed contractor with any required permits pulled and signed off on by the city inspector prior to closing.

Follow up with the other items, with as few bullet points as possible. If you have five plumbing issues, ask for all of them under one bullet. The four electrical issues get one bullet. A long punch list will put the seller (and the listing agent) in a bad mood before they even read it. I once got a two-page inspection notice that was made up mostly of requests for information, such as "Seller to identify the location of the main water shut-off" and "Seller to provide all instruction manuals and warranties to buyer at closing." The buyer only asked for three reasonable repairs, but my seller was so put off by the long "list," she initially balked at even doing those!

Make it easy for the seller to say "yes." Draft your request respectfully and do not imply by the words you choose that the home is in shameful disrepair. Simply state your requests and do not embellish them. For example, do not say, "Seller shall repair the leak under the kitchen sink to avoid further mold and mildew damage to the cabinet, flooring and possibly the basement ceiling." Simply say, "Seller shall repair the leak under the kitchen sink."

The "Inspection From Hell"

Let's play a different game now. Let's pretend we're at a grueling four-hour inspection. Hail damage on the roof, a suspicious crack in the furnace, some structural cracks above windows and doors, evidence of termite damage—and we're just getting started. Stay calm. Watch your buyer's reaction. If he's upset, don't talk him out of it. Assure him that he doesn't have to buy the house if the physical condition is unsatisfactory to him, but that you will do your best to negotiate the repairs if that's what he wants. Whatever you do, don't belittle his concerns; he'll just dig in his heels. Your unconditional support will allow him to evaluate the situation objectively and make the right decision for himself without worrying about your disapproval.

If you have never gone through a difficult inspection before, this may all seem obvious to you, as a soulful real estate agent. Of course you will always support your client's wishes, right? Yes, in an ideal world, you would and you should. But, let's be honest, the world of commissioned sales is far from that utopia. When your commission check is on the line and you're watching your first (or second or third or tenth) sale evaporate before your eyes, you might find yourself doing things your soul would not approve of. It's human nature and I won't pretend that I never did it. I know that I pushed some buyers through a rough inspection out of my own desperation for a closing. It almost always came back to haunt me.

Drafting the Inspection Request for an "Inspection From Hell"

If the home truly is in surprising disrepair (i.e., the buyers weren't intending to buy a fix-up), go ahead and ask the seller to fix everything if that's what your buyers want you to do. Group your objections into categories and keep the language short and simple, not emotional or inflammatory. Include your inspection report if you think further explanation or clarification will be needed. Put some thought into the wording of your objections—don't just copy the inspection report word for word. This gives you, and your request, a little bit more credibility.

Don't be hostile with the listing agent. She wants a closing just as badly as you do and will be your greatest ally if she feels you and your buyers are behaving respectfully.

Keep in mind that the seller wants, and hopefully needs, to sell her house. If she doesn't fix the problems for your buyer, she'll likely have to fix them for the next. Unfortunately, sometimes it takes a seller a few crashed deals to accept reality and it may be the next buyer who benefits from your buyer's experience. But if the seller is motivated and the listing agent is in control of her client, these deals can be salvaged if both parties want it to be.

THE FINAL STRETCH—MOVING TOWARD CLOSING

Okay, if you're through inspection, it's safe to breathe a sigh of relief. The inspection is often the toughest part of a residential home sale. Now the experts take over. That would be the mortgage broker, the title company or

THE TITLE COMPANY
The company that provides title insurance and closing services. The title company handles collection and distribution of funds, conducts the closing and ensures clear title to the buyer.

attorney, and the appraiser. Your job at this point is to ensure that the inspection items are completed as agreed, that the closing is scheduled and that the loan is progressing smoothly.

Buyer Gets Loan Approval

The final contingency is usually loan approval. Hopefully, this requires no more than a few phone calls to the lender to ensure that the loan is on track. Be sure to call the lender on the day before the formal loan approval deadline to see if an extension will be needed, so you can prepare to grovel before the listing agent.

Final Walk-thru

CAUTION!

Be sure to call the listing agent before your walk-thru to confirm that all inspection items are complete; your buyer will be understandably concerned, and you will look clueless and even incompetent if you are surprised by items left undone.

Schedule your final walk-thru with your buyer and the listing agent. The purpose of the walk-thru is to confirm that inspection items have been completed (take your inspection paperwork!), that the sellers appear to be moving out and that the home is in the same condition as it was at inspection, "normal wear and tear excepted."

Closing

Closing protocol is different across the country. In some markets, the buyers and sellers all get together in one room and have a little key exchange party, facilitated by the title company. In others, the buyers and sellers never even meet. In resort markets, it is common that no one attends the closing—all paperwork is done through the mail.

Depending on your local customs, your responsibilities for the closing may include reviewing the closing statement for accuracy, communicating to your buyer the amount and type of funds (cashier's check, wire transfer, etc.) needed to close, ensuring that you have the required signatures on all contracts and disclosures, arranging the key exchange for your buyer and making sure the buyer has documentation for all inspection items requiring proof.

Oh, yes—and collecting your commission check! Woo hoo!

So, that's a general overview of the home-buying process. Now, let's look at a real world example.

REAL ESTATE IN THE REAL WORLD
YOUR FIRST BUYER

Let's say you meet a buyer at your first open house. She's looking for a home similar to the one you held open, but a little less expensive.

During your first serious conversation with a new buyer, you want to get an idea for her buying time frame (right away, in six months, sometime next year), her "must-haves" (number of bedrooms, baths, location, etc.), her price range and her willingness to contact a lender. If she has a lender already (great, she's for real!), get his contact information from her.

The point of the first phone conversation is to build rapport and to inspire confidence in you, not to "qualify" the buyer. You only have a limited amount of time to make a good impression, and if you spend all your time making sure the buyer is suitable to work with, you'll just alienate her.

With that in mind, you need to be truly interested in her and what she wants and needs. Close your eyes and imagine how you would want to treated if you called up a real estate agent, interested in a particular house or neighborhood. You'd probably want the agent to be excited to hear from you. You'd want the agent to sound competent and knowledgeable. You'd want the agent to ask you about you, not tell you about her. You wouldn't want to be sold or closed, especially this early in the process.

The best way to excite a buyer on the phone is to know your market well enough to be able to rev her up about a few houses that might fit her needs. The better you know your market, the easier this will be for you to do, and the higher your conversion ratio (the number of times you turn a prospect into a client) will be. It will come.

During this getting-to-know-you-and-your-needs phone call, try to get on the buyer's calendar. This will motivate you to start preparing and hopefully make the first step toward getting her committed to you. Please don't push her for buyer agency until you've spent some time together and you feel that you're a good fit. We'll discuss buyer agency later in this chapter.

So let's say that she tells you she wants to move in four months, she thinks her maximum price is around $200,000, she needs three bedrooms and two full baths because she wants to get a roommate. She's willing to do a little fix-up, but nothing major like electrical or plumbing. She'd like to live in the neighborhood where you held your open house. With regard to a lender, she's open to your recommendations.

This is all good news. If she needs to move in four months, that means she needs to have a home under contract no later than three months from today, preferably in two and a half months. It sounds like a long time, but it isn't. Assuming her price range is reasonable (we'll find out soon!), she sounds like a darn near perfect buyer. We'll see....

If she's not sure of a price range, encourage her to talk to a lender right away. As in, today. You don't want to waste her time showing homes she can't afford. Conversely, many times buyers will raise their price range after talking with a lender. If a buyer has not spoken with a lender, she really has no idea what her price range should be.

You schedule your first date on Saturday. Let's say today is Tuesday. That's plenty of time, but we need to get started.

Search for Homes

Let's head to the MLS. Search for homes with a minimum of three bedrooms and two baths, priced from $170,000 to $210,000 (always search a little above your buyer's maximum; we'll discuss this in a little bit), in her preferred neighborhood. For this first showing tour, you want to show her truly wonderful homes that meet or beat her criteria, if her criteria is reasonable.

What if it's not? What if she can't afford the house she says she wants?

If her criteria is not reasonable, here's what you need to do. Typically, the problem will be price for the location. In other words, she wants a neighborhood she can't afford. Before you call her to discuss this dilemma, think of other neighborhoods that offer similar amenities and general ambience. If she's looking for a newer home on the west side of town, search the MLS listings by Year of Construction (along with her "must-haves") to find other possibilities. If you know nothing about the neighborhoods you find, make a little road trip to see if they are good alternatives to her preferred neighborhood.

You also need to know what she can have in her price range in her preferred neighborhood. Maybe a three bedroom home isn't reasonable, but a two bedroom home is. Don't be surprised if she's completely priced out of her neighborhood; this happens a lot with buyers you meet at open houses. Open house shoppers tend to hunt for homes in the nicest neighborhoods, which they often can't afford.

That's a bit of a buzz-kill, isn't it? Unfortunately, it's common. Regardless of your buyer's price range (even if it's in the millions), buyers always want what they just can't quite have. But if you can "solve her problem," you'll still sell her a house.

JENNIFER'S $0.02

Most buyers claim to be "open to fix-ups," yet very few truly are. So disregard her comments about her willingness to "do a little work" until you've shown her homes and can judge for yourself.

PreviewPreviewPreview

Anyway, back to the MLS. Let's assume that you find some decent homes in her preferred neighborhood, with all her requirements. Go preview as many as you can right away. You're looking for the best 6-10 homes to show her on Saturday. By "best," I mean...first and foremost, they show well. They're clean, well decorated and smell good. They don't have any fatal flaws, especially locational fatal flaws (e.g., they don't back to a grocery store). They meet all or most of her needs. They have good street appeal.

If you find enough great homes on your first preview trip, that's excellent! If you don't, branch out and preview in similar near-by neighborhoods. Even if you do find enough good homes in her preferred neighborhood, I'd highly recommend previewing in alternative neighborhoods anyway so that you can speak intelligently about her alternatives. Market Knowledge...Market

Knowledge...Market Knowledge...will make you money.

If the top of her price range is $200,000, go ahead and select a few homes slightly above that mark (make sure they're nearly perfect), but keep the majority of the homes you show within her stated price range. If you only show her houses at the top of her range or above, she'll wonder if you're pushing her to spend more so that you'll make a larger commission check. Buyers do think this way.

Set Your Showings

Depending on protocol in your market, set up your showings early. If you're showing on Saturday morning, set your showings early Friday afternoon. Plan your route; if you're showing in an unfamiliar neighborhood, go drive your route. You'll be glad you did when you're in the car with your buyer. Print out full-color informational sheets for your buyer for each listing and put them in the order you'll be showing them. Your own showing sheets will also be in the proper order with the lockbox and/or showing instructions written on each.
If you have to pick up keys to show properties, allow plenty of time to do this before your appointment. Don't be running around picking up keys with your buyer in the car. Even if other agents do it, I think it makes you look unprepared.

Don't forget to wash your car!!!

Meet Your Buyer!

You can meet the buyer at your office or some other convenient location. Put her in your (clean) car; don't let her follow you in hers unless she has a small child in a car seat. This is critical rapport-building time.

JENNIFER'S $0.02

Many agents are uncomfortable putting strangers in their car and prefer to have their buyers drive themselves. Obviously, your safety is far more important than rapport-building, so follow your gut when making this decision.

Give her the MLS printouts, let her review them. Explain the process of looking at homes. I always ask "Have you ever looked at homes with a real estate agent before?" If she has, she probably doesn't need too much prepping. If she hasn't, I tell her several things about the process, specifically...that she probably will only like a few of the homes we look at...that she will know the right house when she sees it...that she is free to look in closets, pantries, kitchen cupboards ...that hopefully the seller won't be home, but if he is, just to do her best to pretend he's not.

Showing Homes

Let the buyer discover the home on her own. Buyers don't need an agent's help finding the kitchen or the back yard. Don't chatter at her or point out all the special features. If she likes the feel of a house, she'll start looking for special features and then you can help. If the house doesn't warm her toes, your observations and opinions aren't going to change her mind. You cannot sell a buyer on a house. Don't try, it will just annoy her.

Please be sure to lock up the home properly when you leave. I once showed a home to a party of five (the buyer and his family), and in all the chaos, we left the back patio door wide open. Unfortunately, my buyer loved this home, but the seller was so upset with me that he initially rejected my buyer's offer!

Ask your buyer for her thoughts every time you return to your car. Toward the end of her tour, ask her if you're on the right track or if you should change gears a bit. (This is where previewing alternative neighborhoods can really help you sound professional.) Did you get a feel for her fix-up tolerance? Talk to her about her conversation with the lender.

After you've shown her the last home, try to get her perspective on the day. I always say, "Well, that's our show for today. How did we do?"

After the Tour...

If you looked at more than six homes, she might be feeling overwhelmed and worn out. Looking at homes is hard work! Don't push her for opinions if she seems a little dazed. Don't make a big deal about planning another date with you.

But on the other hand, don't just let her go. Make sure she knows you enjoyed spending time with her and that you're looking forward to doing it again, at her convenience. If she has particular interest in a home or two, promise her that you'll get more information for her.

Buyers who are interested in a home always want to know the seller's motivation and what they originally paid for the home. You might be able to convince the listing agent to divulge the first, and the second should be public record. This gives you a good excuse to call your buyer back right away. At that time, you can offer your services for a second trip.

Buyer Agency

Not to be confused with a required agency disclosure, a buyer agency agreement obligates the buyer to the agent for a specified period of time. If the buyer purchases a home during the contract period, the buyer is contractually agreeing to ensure that his agent gets a commission on that home. Once a buyer signs a buyer agency agreement, he is bound to that agent. If he purchases a home using another agent, he may be obligated to pay both agents a commission.

Personally, I put off the buyer agency conversation as long as I legally can. Your broker may require you to discuss it up front and there are good legal reasons for this. I just don't agree with the concept that you should force yourself on a virtual stranger before you know if the two of you are a good fit for each other. I'm not giving legal advice here, but try to have a casual discussion about agency with your buyer during your first tour together. If your company requires a signed disclosure statement from your buyer, by all means, comply.

Practice your agency disclosure speech so that it flows naturally. If you are uncomfortable with it, your buyer will wonder why. And will be uncomfortable too.

If you have the attitude that anyone would be lucky to have you on his team while shopping for a house, it's pretty easy to discuss buyer agency. But note, I said "discuss," not "bully."

You can say, "At some point, you'll need to decide if you want to hire me as your buyer agent. I won't push you to do it—it's your decision, but the State of Colorado (insert your state) requires that we formalize our relationship..."

Your Second, Third and Fourth (?) Trips

Hopefully your first showing tour went so well that you have another one scheduled. Now you have a better idea of what she likes, so you'll have more fun previewing for her. Why? It's WAY more fun to preview with a purpose. You're looking for your buyer's Dream House! When you find it...it feels great.

It may take two trips, three trips, eight trips, twenty trips...to find your buyer's home. There are lots of variables that affect how many homes you have to show...buyer motivation, fussiness or indecisiveness, your skill as a buyer agent, the inventory and, of course, luck. Hang in there.

Stay on top of new listings for your buyer. Look every single day; if it's a strong seller's market, several times a day. Call her or e-mail her every time you see something good. Preview new listings as often as you can. In short, work your ass off for this first buyer. You'll be a much stronger agent for it.

Making an Offer

We covered this topic extensively earlier, but here are a few additional comments.

Once you've written and submitted your offer, your buyer will be waiting by the phone for your call. Stay in touch with her. Actually, I probably don't have to tell you this—you'll be just as anxious as she is! I remember making the comment early in my career that I could never sell real estate if I were single... to be constantly waiting by the phone for both business AND love? I'd lose my mind.

Anyway, even if you have no news, call her to tell her that. If she's waiting by the phone for your call...and it doesn't come...she'll get a little hostile. It's not personal, it's just the strong emotions of buying a home coming to the surface.

If the seller rejects or counters her offer, your buyer will be disappointed. Be disappointed with her. Don't imply that "you told her so" if she made a lowball offer against your judgment.

Hopefully, she will ask you for your advice. The best answer is, "Well, what do you want to do?" Does she still want the home? Or is she already having buyer's remorse before even buying anything? If she still wants the home, explain her options (accept the counterproposal or write a new offer). If she is wavering, let her stew on it. Don't push her unless you sense that she truly wants to be pushed.

That said, some buyers need you to make decisions for them. If you can't get a straight answer out of her, offer some suggestions. Such as, "Why don't we write a new offer at $195,000 and ask for the refrigerator?" She might jump on that idea. If so, great. Write it up.

Sometimes a negotiation gets hot and heavy. Phone calls burning up the lines between the listing and buyer agents with offers and counter-offers and counter-offers to the counter-offer. "$198,500 with no refrigerator," "$193,000 with the refrigerator," "$197,000 with the refrigerator," "$194,000."

When this happens, a great strategy is to suddenly withdraw from the negotiation. Advise your buyer to sit tight over-night and let the sellers worry that they went too far. Don't return the last call from the listing agent for several hours. Finally, call her back and tell her your buyer is thinking about it. Tell her you'll call her sometime tomorrow. This works like a charm with the sellers. Of course, another offer could come in and kill the whole thing and you need to tell your buyer this. But if she's stuck on price, this is the best way to get it for her. It also slows her down so she doesn't get caught up in the negotiation...and have buyer's remorse next week (for which she'll blame YOU!).

If you can't put the deal together...your buyer may need a break. Rarely does she want to hit the streets again right away, unless she's in a time crunch. Part of this is emotional, part of it is real life. She's put her life on hold the last few days and she may have an overflowing in-box at home or work. Let her regroup if she needs to.

Surprisingly, if she had a second choice home, she probably won't be remotely interested in it now. I don't know why, but when buyers have an unsuccessful negotiation, they rarely will consider any of the homes they've already looked at. They need to start fresh.

But let's not think about that right now. Let's think positive and assume the negotiation was successful.

Congratulations!

CHECKLIST FOR BUYERS UNDER CONTRACT

Here is the first of several checklists for you! This checklist addresses the items that are your responsibility during the period from contract to closing, as the buyer agent. A simpler version of the checklist without my commentary is available in the Appendix and on my website. It is formatted to be used as a check-off sheet for each buyer if you aren't yet using a contract management program.

IMMEDIATELY AFTER CONTRACT IS EXECUTED

✓ Put contract dates in your contract manager program
Important dates include any objection deadlines (inspection, insurance, title, covenant review, appraisal, etc.), loan approval or any other agreements made in the contract. If you don't use a contract management program, enter these dates in your planner.

✓ Fax the executed contract and copy of earnest money to the buyer's lender

✓ Deliver the property disclosures to your buyer and get signatures

✓ Deliver earnest money check to listing agent, if not already done

✓ Give the buyer the HOA contact and questionnaire
Do so if applicable. See Chapter Twelve for more information on the questionnaire.

✓ Advise the buyer to schedule the inspection(s)

FIRST WEEK AFTER CONTRACT EXECUTION

✓ Call the buyer's lender to confirm loan application

✓ Ask buyer's lender to delay appraisal until after the inspection period
If the appraisal is ordered too soon, a chance exists that the appraiser will complete the appraisal before the inspection is

successfully negotiated. If the buyer terminates the contract due to inspection issues, he could still be charged for the appraisal. I always try to head this off with the lender.

✓ Deliver signed property disclosures to listing agent

✓ Advise the buyer to look into hazard insurance

✓ Call buyer's lender to check in

✓ Schedule the closing (after inspection is resolved)

10 DAYS TO ONE WEEK PRIOR TO CLOSING

✓ Arrange Power of Attorney or mail-out close, if applicable
If your buyer will not attend closing, make sure the title company and lender are aware of this way ahead of time. Either the buyer will need to designate someone to sign for him (and it shouldn't be you), or the entire package will be mailed or e-mailed to him. Typically, the title company will coordinate this for you, as long as they know about it.

✓ Confirm that the inspection items are complete—ask for documentation

✓ Schedule the walk-thru

✓ Are there any changes that need to be communicated to the lender or title company?
Many times, contract provisions will be changed or negotiated and no one remembers to let the lender and/or title company know. If material changes are a surprise to the lender or title company, you may not have a closing when you planned!

✓ Remind the buyer to call utility companies to transfer service (provide phone numbers)

1 - 2 DAYS BEFORE CLOSING

✓ Confirm with all parties the closing date, time and place

✓ Review the closing statement

At least half the time the closing statement will have an error or two. Review it closely. Don't forget any negotiated credits for closing costs or inspection items. Ensure that the earnest money has been credited. If you haven't yet received a closing statement from the lender or title company, call to find out why.

✓ Call the buyer with closing figures

After you have blessed the closing figures, call your buyer to let her know how much money she needs to bring to the closing. Make sure she knows that her funds need to be in the form of a cashiers check, not a personal check! Remind her to bring identification.

✓ Prepare the file for closing

Ensure that all documents and disclosures are signed. Review the contract and any amendments to refresh your memory on items to be confirmed prior to closing. Make sure the file is organized so that you will be able to quickly answer any questions that may arise at closing. If your office provides a list of required documents that you must turn in after closing (to get your paycheck), review the checklist and take it with you.

AFTER CLOSING

✓ Turn in the closed file to the office manager

...so you get paid!

✓ Update your buyer's address in your SOI manager

✓ Add buyer to your post closing follow up plan

I have a follow-up plan that reminds me to send greeting cards to my clients at intervals after closing. I send a card one month, six months, one year, two years and three years after closing. I don't necessarily send "Happy Six Month" anniversary cards, just something to let them know I still exist and am still in real estate. Sometimes I'll send a little gift, like a $10 Starbucks gift card, just thanking them again for their business.

✓ Call buyer a few days after move in

> *Don't be accused of getting your commission check and disappearing off the face of the earth. This is definitely Old School behavior! Usually the buyer is thrilled with her new home, but if a problem has arisen, this is a golden opportunity for you to help. It may be contrary to your natural instincts to go looking for trouble, but the bonus points you'll rack up are worth the extra hassle.*

> *I once worked with a first-time buyer who was so nervous about buying a home that he literally got the flu right before closing. The thought of being a homeowner with homeowner responsibilities was just about more than he could handle. He did close however and I breathed a sigh of relief. When I called him a few days after closing to check in, he said that the outlet for the dryer didn't work and he was in a panic. He asked me if I would call the previous owner and get him to fix it. I was all set to explain to him that once he closed on the house, these sorts of problems would come up and he'd have to deal with them. Luckily, my more soulful instincts kicked in and I stopped myself. I called the previous owner and amazingly, he sent over his handyman right away to fix the plug. Problem solved. Don't be afraid of reasonable requests' every once in a while you'll be pleasantly surprised and maybe even look like a hero. Especially to those nervous first-time buyers.*

CLOSING GIFTS

For years I spent hours coming up with the perfect gift for each of my wonderful clients. It was probably one of the biggest time and money wasters in my business. First, closings are a hectic time for buyers and sellers. They are in the process of uprooting their lives and they have a lot on their minds. Sure, your closing gift is nice, but it's just not going to get the attention it deserves at this particular time. It might just be one more thing they have to pack and move.

A much better idea is to contact the client a month or so later and make arrangements to drop off a gift, if you must. Because initiating social encounters is intimidating for me, just calling a client to say hi does not come naturally. Having an excuse to call (i.e., to drop off my fabulous closing gift) makes it much easier for me. If "warm-calling" comes naturally for you, you really don't need the gift, just yourself.

your first listing appointment

Yippee! You Have Your First Listing Appointment!
Yikes! You Have Your First Listing Appointment!

Your Listing Presentation

Thinking back, I recall that I was a little embarrassed by the boilerplate material that my Big Name company provided me to use on listings. I thought it was patronizing to the client and didn't reflect who I really was. I don't think I ever used it, even on my very first listing appointment. If the listing proposal material that is provided by your company resonates with you, by all means use it.

Instead, I created my own written listing proposal. It says what I want it to say, how I want to say it, and I feel that it assumes a level of intelligence on the part of my seller prospect. Home sellers may sit through three or more listing proposals before they hire an agent, so I feel it is my duty to cut out the fluff and propaganda, and get directly to the point—that is, what I think the house is worth, what I'm going to do to sell it and how much I'm going to charge.

Some agents take the reduction of fluff and propaganda to the extreme. I've seen more than one Top Dog agent race out the door, late for a listing appointment, a pile of MLS printouts in hand. This is their listing proposal. Clearly it works for them and they must have the confidence and charisma to pull it off, although I think it's disrespectful to the client.

Not being particularly charismatic, I need the crutch and support of a well-prepared listing proposal. My prospects are always impressed with how professional and thorough my presentations are and I know they appreciate the time I take putting them together.

My written listing proposal consists of two major sections. The first (the marketing proposal) is an introduction to me, my services and my fees. The second is the market analysis or CMA.

Section One (The Marketing Proposal)

Marketing Services: A summary of the services I provide my selling clients. Includes both pre-contract (marketing) and post-contract (closing) services.

My Fee: A one page description of my listing fee.

Samples of Marketing: Internet pages, color brochures, newspaper ads, etc.

My Bragging Rights: A list of homes sold, awards, newspaper clippings.

Section Two (The CMA)

Your Property: A printout of the county assessor page for their home. I also include the prior MLS listing of the home if it has been listed in the last three years.

Current Competition: Comparable Listings—similar homes for sale in the immediate neighborhood.

Other Competition—similar homes for sale outside of the immediate neighborhood, but comparable in appeal.

Recent Sales: All Recent Neighborhood Sales (not just the comparable homes). Recent

	Comparable Sales—the ten or so homes that have recently sold in the same general price range as the prospect.
	Most Comparable Sales—the three or so homes that you will be using to price this home.
Pending Sales:	A simple list of the homes showing as "under contract."
Expired Listings:	The comparable homes that did not sell.
Estimate of Market Value:	You will want to provide a pricing recommendation backed up by solid data, in an easy-to-understand format.
Estimated Cost of Sale:	Otherwise known as a "net sheet." To calculate the estimated cost of sale, you take the projected sales price less the commission and any other fees the seller pays, such as a title policy, recording fees, closing fees or HOA transfer fees. (If you have not yet determined a market value for the home, you can still do a net sheet. Just use a nice round number and make sure your prospect knows it's for "illustrative purposes" only.)

You do not have to review all this data line by line with the seller. You just want to show the seller you have done your homework, and that you are a professional. He can review it at his leisure. Even if he really doesn't care about all the market data, he will appreciate the effort you took preparing it for him.

Once you get the hang of it, you'll be able to put most of the presentation together in your sleep. The trick is knowing your software well enough to trust the data it gives you. Nothing is worse than driving to your prospect's home for the listing interview and seeing For Sale signs in front of comparable homes that didn't make your list. Bad, very bad for your confidence.

Proper Pricing is Your Duty

One of the most important duties of your job is to properly price your listings for market. Getting listings is one thing, selling them is another. Sure, it's fun to see your name on a sign in a yard, but yard signs don't pay the bills. There is a right way to price a home, which involves a thorough review of the market—the active competition, the recent sales and the expired listings. The wrong way is to allow your seller to dictate the price. Not that you don't want her input, but you need to know in your heart what the right price range is and be able to defend it.

You know how they say that you learn the most from the challenges in your life? The good stuff rarely teaches you anything and the most valuable lessons come from your mistakes and missteps. I could take up the rest of this book telling you why and how not to take overpriced listings, but you will do it anyway. We all do. However, as you mature in your real estate career, you will learn how to say no—to either turn down a listing or tactfully convince your seller to see things your way.

Believe it or not, there are lots of Old School agents out there who don't particularly care if their listings sell or not. They just want to blanket the town with their signs and will do whatever it takes to procure yet another listing, which often includes overpricing their listings to "win" the seller's business. However, what they forget is that, as licensed professional real estate agents, it is their duty to be honest and straightforward with their sellers about market value. Our job as real estate agents is not to make friends because we are the highest bidder. Sellers are depending on us and our recommendations in order to make important decisions.

JENNIFER'S BLOG
Is It Okay to Take an Overpriced Listing so You Can Acquire Buyer Leads?

No! It's not okay to take an overpriced listing just so you can acquire leads. We were not granted a real estate license by our state's real estate division so we could master the art of lead generation; we are licensed so that we can professionally assist the public with their real estate needs.

Page one of the Code of Ethics and Standards of Practice of the National Association of Realtors® actually states pretty darn clearly that: "Realtors®, in attempting to secure a listing, shall not deliberately mislead the owner as to market value." So someone thinks it's pretty important! We are not For-Sale-Signs-For-Hire; we are supposedly professionals who have more knowledge and expertise than our clients and should be trusted to share that knowledge with them.

Besides, don't kid yourself. Once your sign goes in that yard with a too-high price, it will be All Your Fault when it doesn't sell. It doesn't matter how many disclosures you made or how much money you got up front for advertising, your seller will blame you when the home doesn't sell.

It's easy to forget this. To forget that we are hired by sellers to do a job, part of which might include telling them something they don't want to hear. In my opinion (and the opinion of your real estate commission), misleading a seller with respect to the marketability of her home is unethical. Ignorance of the market is no excuse. If you don't know (and are not willing to learn) the nuances of a particular market, you have no business going on that listing appointment. Real estate is not about you and your needs! Don't forget this!

Agents who take overpriced listings do a huge disservice to their clients – who they have committed (in writing on a legal document) to look out for.

Pricing listings right is an art and a skill that, once mastered, will make your life as a real estate agent much more pleasant, productive and profitable. All of us have taken overpriced listings and most of us swore we'd never do it again. But of course we do.

However, to take a listing you know is overpriced simply to get leads is in violation of your duty to your seller. In my humble opinion.

The "Art" of Pricing Homes

Between you and me, pricing a home is an art, not a science. While there certainly are objective parameters to help you price a home (square footage, bedrooms, baths, lot size, etc.), the final buying decision is almost always based on emotion. If there are two identical homes on the same block for sale and one smells good, looks good and feels good, and the other is smoky, poorly furnished and hard to show, there is a difference in market value, which may be hard to objectively demonstrate.

JENNIFER'S $0.02...

I firmly believe that if you don't work with buyers on a regular basis, you don't have the expertise to accurately price homes for market. Many experienced agents snottily declare that they Don't Work With Buyers—they only handle listings and hire buyer agents to show homes. I know a few agents in my area who are huge listers and have never shown or previewed one of my listings. I don't understand how they can claim to be the neighborhood experts when they don't know the competition and don't have an understanding of how buyers think.

Your clients and prospects look at you as the expert. In reality, there is no way to accurately and scientifically place a value on a home; a lot depends on market conditions (that week!), luck, and even the weather. But sellers understandably want you (the expert) to tell them exactly what their home is worth. So, I do my best to give them as much hard data as I can to justify my pricing recommendation.

What if You Underprice a Home?

Sellers almost always want to "try" a higher listing price than I recommend. When I acquiesce, I always regret it.

So why do I do it? Because I'm afraid of underpricing the home. Believe me, there's nothing fun about receiving multiple offers on a brand new listing (unless that's normal for your market). Your seller is initially excited, but soon enough he'll be looking askance at you with the unspoken (if you're lucky) accusation that you underpriced his home. Never mind that he probably got a higher sales price than he expected, never mind that his worries about languishing on the market were unfounded—you cost him money.

This has happened to me twice. Both times, I was confident that my pricing recommendation was accurate, but for whatever reason, the market responded to the listing more positively than I expected. Fortunately, both times, the homes sold in bidding wars for much higher than the listed price. However, it was uncomfortable enough for me to still question myself every time I price a home. In fact, I often breathe a sigh of relief 48 hours after putting a home on the market that it didn't sell in a bidding war.

I'll never forget the scolding I received the last time I underpriced a home. My market analysis showed a value of $408,000 to $419,000, but the house showed so well, I agreed to try $425,000. The first day on the market, we had eight showings and four offers. Ouch.

We put the home under contract at $441,000. My sellers got everything they wanted, including a rent-back agreement that heavily favored the sellers. I figured they would be happy. I should have known better.

A few days later, I had to apologize to my seller for some miscommunication with my showing service and during my apology phone call, my seller said, "And Jennifer, we've never discussed how you grossly underpriced our home. Obviously you didn't do your homework and I'm disappointed in you. Just so you know, we don't intend to fix anything at the inspection or be flexible in any way with these buyers." Talk about a buzz-kill.

At the risk of sounding like sour grapes, it's impossible to explain to sellers that, had they priced the home higher, they would probably have ended up at the same sales price, only after a longer marketing period and more disruption in their lives. They don't understand how painful it is to fall into the death spiral where you can't reduce the price fast enough as the listing gets stale.

My recommendation? You're better off taking the chance of underpricing a home than overpricing it. Keep in mind that in ten years, I only underpriced two homes. But I overpriced plenty and everyone suffered. No one wins when a home is overpriced. Especially not the seller.

Selling real estate is not always fun. But most of the time it is.

Five Steps to the Right Price

If you are a new agent, be prepared to spend several hours on your first listing presentations. As you gain expertise, you should be able to put together a market analysis in an hour or two. But in the beginning, the more time you spend in preparation, the more confident you will be going to your appointment. Here are the steps to follow each and every time you price a home for market.

1. Drive by the Home

It doesn't matter how well you know the subject property's neighborhood, you must not skip this step. More often than not you will be surprised by what you see. A gas station across the alley, an overbuilt home next door blocking the light, a hideous enclosed sun porch...or perhaps the home suffers from excessive highway noise. Drive around the block to identify the other homes for sale in the immediate area. You must know the price and status of these homes before you step foot into your listing prospect's home.

One evening I had a listing appointment for a home outside of my comfort zone. I had never been anywhere near the neighborhood, but I was an "experienced" agent at this point and figured I could wing it. I prepared my market analysis without driving by the home and was fairly confident as I drove to my appointment.

My confidence started to fade as I saw lots of For Sale signs within a few blocks of my prospect. None of these properties were shown on my market analysis and I had no idea how they were priced. I was a little bit early, so I frantically started calling the listing offices of these homes, trying to get as much information as I could so I wouldn't look like a complete idiot with my prospect. As you can imagine, all I managed to accomplish was to increase my anxiety to the point I considered canceling the appointment all together.

What I did instead was take out the market analysis section of my listing presentation with the promise to return the next day with the information "now that I'd seen their home." I didn't get the listing, and I suspect it was due partly to my lack of confidence upon meeting the seller. Moral of the story—you must be confident in the quality and thoroughness of your market data.

2. Find Your Market Data

This might be harder than you think. In many MLS systems, it can be difficult to isolate the homes in a given area that you need to use as comparable properties. Depending on your city, you can use North/South - East/West boundaries, neighborhood names, school district or zip codes. However, many times these pieces of information are subject to mistakes or omissions in input by the listing agent or the office staff. Your goal is to produce a comprehensive list of every single home that is available or has recently sold within the area of the subject property. It is embarrassing and deflating when your prospect asks you about a recent sale down the street that you don't know anything about. Your credibility and confidence take an unneeded hit.

CAUTION!

You need to realize that the MLS is loaded with mistakes and erroneous information. Either the information is entered by the listing agents themselves (who by nature aren't usually detail fanatics) or by the office manager, who hasn't seen the home.

In the Denver market, for example, the best way I have found to search for comparable properties is to search by street name and address number. In my MLS search, I input the street names of the ten streets to the east and west of my subject property, along with address numbers ten blocks north and south (that's the way the Denver grid is laid out). I get all the homes in the immediate area and am not dependent on the listing agent's accurate data input. Errors abound in MLS listings, but you can usually count on the property street name and address number being correct.

If your MLS or your subject area's layout makes this search strategy impractical, try to find a search parameter that is not dependent upon the listing agent's discretion. Never use the neighborhood name if the listing agent has any control over that field. Given the opportunity, agents will always try to "upgrade" the location of their listings to a swankier neighborhood.

3. Preview All Active Listings Competing with the Subject Property

Don't miss any homes in the immediate area...and fan out as time permits. Take notes on the listing printout. If you have already seen the interior of the subject home, rate the properties against it (e.g., "Nicer than," "Better location than," etc.). Your seller prospect may have already seen these homes too, either at open houses or neighborhood events, so you need to be familiar with the interiors of as many nearby listings as you can.

4. Print Out and Drive by the Solds in the Immediate Area

Since these homes have already sold, obviously you can't preview them. Do the best you can with the exterior appearance and the MLS comments. Note which homes are most similar in appeal and location.

5. Review Your Data and Determine the Market Value Range

The results of your research will be entered into the Market Analysis section of your listing presentation. As you are preparing the analysis, you will start to narrow in on a price range for the property. It just happens naturally. This is why I can't imagine having anyone else prepare my market analyses. It is your job as the real estate agent to know the market and to be comfortable educating your seller on current market values. The process of preparing a market analysis is as much for you as for the client.

Put it all together and voilá! You have a CMA!

THE TWO MOST INTIMIDATING CONVERSATIONS IN REAL ESTATE

There are two sensitive topics to be discussed in a listing presentation. One is your commission. I'll cover that topic fully a little later. The other is your pricing recommendation for the home.

Discussing Price with Your Seller Prospect

Most of the time, your seller prospect thinks his home is worth more than you do. Or, even if he agrees with you (in theory) he still wants to test the market, just in case you're both wrong. Popular seller arguments are:

> "I don't want to leave money on the table."
> "I'm not in a hurry."
> "But I need $xx,xxx to make it worth selling."
> "Buyers can always make an offer."

You will hear these statements over and over. In fact, when you sell your own home, you'll laugh when you hear your very own voice making the same arguments.

Let's counter each objection individually.

"I don't want to leave money on the table"

My Response: I understand and I don't want to give away your money. However, the risk of leaving money on the table is slim, almost non-existent. If we accidentally or even intentionally underprice your home, the market will recognize it as a bargain and your home will sell at market value, even if that market value is higher than our asking price. In my ten years of selling real estate, I have only underpriced two homes and both times the home sold above the asking price with multiple offers.

"But I'm not in a hurry!"

My Response: Our goal needs to be a 30-day sale—that's what we're shooting for. The quicker your home sells, the higher your sales price will be. After 30 days on the market, listings become stale and are considered fair game for low-ball offers by buyers. There is an energy in a new listing that quickly fades after a month. Would you be willing to pay full price for a home that has been on the market for 63 days? For 122 days?

"I need $xxx,xxx to make it worth selling" or "I won't sell if I can't walk away with $xx,xxx in my pocket."

My Response: I understand. So here's an idea. Why don't we hold off on listing the home right now and, when the market improves, we'll list it then? I'd be happy to stay in touch with you in the meantime and when I see enough appreciation in the market I'll let you know right away.

(This is a brilliant strategy. It subtly tells the seller that you are willing to walk away from his listing without coming right out and saying so. You aren't beating up the seller by telling him (again) that his price is too high, just that the timing might not be quite right. Somehow this strategy elevates you to a consultant status rather than a desperate salesperson. Don't worry, he won't want to wait to sell his home unless he truly isn't motivated—in which case, you probably don't even want the listing.)

"Buyers can always make an offer."

My Response: That's true. But the risk we run is that the right buyer for your home will never see it, much less make an offer on it. The perfect buyer for your home is probably looking in a lower price range because that's what he can afford. He might have been thrilled with the features of your home, but since it's out of his price range, his agent won't show it to him. On the flip side, the buyers in a higher price range are looking for more house—that is, they want, and can afford, more features than your home offers. They won't make an offer on your home because it doesn't suit their needs.

CAUTION!

Use the above responses judiciously. You don't want to antagonize your seller by appearing argumentative or implying that he's an idiot. If you get all four objections in one conversation, perhaps just address one or two in detail and simply smile sympathetically as if to say, "I know, I know, what can we do?" at the others.

Your responses are best delivered with the attitude that the question/objection is an excellent one, one that you've never heard before. Respond thoughtfully and respectfully. Bringing your seller around to your point of view without his realizing that you led him there is truly in his best interest. Try to put yourself in a seller's shoes. He wants the highest price for his home, of course, who wouldn't? But he may not understand that the best way to get the highest price is to price the home fairly at the very beginning. It's up to you to make him see this without alienating him.

If you are a born salesperson, this may come naturally to you. Good for you. If you're like the rest of us, it will take practice and a confidence in your market knowledge. If you're a new or newer agent, you probably don't have that yet. It will come and is something to look forward to.

What will help you tremendously is to truly feel in your heart that you don't need this listing. That the seller is not doing you a favor by hiring you—you are bringing your expertise to the table and if the seller does not agree with your professional analysis of the situation, that's fine with you! When a seller sees that you're willing to stick to your guns and cheerfully walk away from his business, his attitude toward you shifts—you'll find that he begins to see you as the expert—it's a beautiful thing. And if he doesn't, it's a listing you probably don't want, no matter how desperate for business you think you are.

Negotiating Your Commission

Fourteen months into my career, I listed a home (the seller picked the price and the 4% commission) and I marketed it hard (it was my second or third listing ever). It was an adorable home on a great lot and it sold quickly at full price. We got through the inspection with no problems. Then, on the day before I was leaving town for my honeymoon—the house didn't appraise. The appraiser's value was about $8,000 lower than the sales price and, on paper, he was right. "Adorable," as you may know, doesn't impress an appraiser.

I didn't know what to do. I really didn't. I argued, I begged, I tried to charm the appraiser, and he was sympathetic, but I didn't give him anything to work with. It appeared that my seller was going to have to reduce her sales price by $8,000 to get the house to closing. She was not amused. At that point, she made the comment, "Well, I guess I got what I paid for," referring to me and my low commission. And you know what? She was right. I didn't have the experience to solve the problem.

But a more experienced agent did. The appraiser (God bless him) took pity on me (after all I was getting married in a few days) and called another agent he knew who did a lot of business in the neighborhood. The other agent was familiar with my listing (I'm sure he interviewed for it) and was able to give the appraiser information about the sold comparables that enabled him to raise his appraised value to the sales price. Whew! Right?

Yes, I dodged a bullet. The home closed and we all moved on. An interesting epilogue to this story—the owner of the home went on to get her real estate license and is quite successful. I'm certain that when people ask her why she went into real estate, she tells them the story about her clueless real estate agent (me) and how she knew she could do better.

So here's my point...

If you are a new real estate salesperson, I don't care how enthusiastic, how smart, how cute, how motivated you are, you are not as qualified to handle the marketing and sale of a home as a good, experienced real estate agent. Now, you might be more qualified than a bad experienced agent, and there are plenty of those. But, be honest, if you were going to hire someone to sell your home (or invest your money, design your logo or walk your dog), would you really prefer someone who has never done it before over an experienced professional?

Every agent goes through a rookie year. Somehow we convince people to give us the listing on their homes, and, in most cases, everything comes out okay. At the end of the year, you can breathe a sigh of relief that you'll never have to be a rookie real estate agent again.

But until then, here's what I think new agents should do. You need listings—you need the inventory to attract buyers and you need the experience. Buy them. The listings, I mean. No, I don't mean you should overprice them (although you'll do that too). Be the lowest bidder on your commission. Your broker might not agree with me, but here's why I think it's a good idea.

First, it's fair to the seller. You don't have the experience or expertise of a 5-year, 10-year or 25-year agent. Don't argue with me, you don't. If a reasonable listing fee in your area is 6%, you aren't worth that yet. Maybe you're worth 4%. Maybe you should even consider working for free for a while; after all, most professions require you to actually pay money to learn a trade, don't they? Ever heard of internships or residencies or apprenticeships? You could simply charge your sellers a marketing fee of, say, $300, which will cover your advertising costs.

You also could creatively market yourself as a first-year real estate agent building a business at a discounted commission. You don't have to come right out and tell sellers that you're learning the ropes at their expense, but they'll realize that, and might even cut you a little slack. After all, if they want a more experienced agent, they can pay for him.

Second, it will help you build your confidence to charge more when you feel you're worth it. I took a lot of 4% commissions my first few years because I didn't have the confidence in my knowledge or my competency to negotiate a higher fee. And I figured a little paycheck is better than no paycheck. Now I have no problem stating my fee and explaining why I am worth it, and I usually get the listing—if I want it.

How to Completely Eliminate Any Fee Negotiation

Even as you gain experience, commission negotiation may be an ongoing issue for you. Here's a strategy that worked beautifully in my business; maybe it will make things easier for you.

Offer your sellers a choice in fee structure, rather than one fee that they suspect is negotiable. I think sellers are just as uncomfortable discussing a brokerage fee as you are presenting it. They know they're supposed to negotiate the commission and they want to feel they got the best deal. So, you are automatically starting off the relationship with the seller as an adversary instead of a partner.

Give your clients an option. They can pay your full commission (let's say 6%), which includes all marketing, advertising and services you describe in your proposal. If you don't sell the home, you don't get paid. Alternatively, they can pay you a reduced commission (let's say 5.2%) with a non-refundable $300 marketing fee, paid at the time of listing. Their choice. Present these options to them up front, maybe before you even meet. It's Sales Tactic #131, "Give people an alternative rather than a straight yes or no proposition."

I think this way is fair to everyone. If you do the math, you'll see that the 5.2% + $300 option will save the seller money and put fewer dollars in your pocket at the end of the day. But the majority of your marketing expenses are paid up front, so if the home does not sell, you've only wasted your time, not your money. And sellers will understand that. You're sharing the risk with your sellers, thus taking a little bit less of a paycheck.

I had great feedback from my sellers on this plan. The discussion over my fee usually took place between the sellers before I even arrived for my appointment and by the time I got there, the sellers told me which plan they preferred. Done—we could move on to less adversarial topics.

When You "Double-End" a Sale...

In real estate, "double-ending" refers to selling your own listing. You "double -end-the-deal" by getting both sides of the commission. Yeah, it's cool. But watch out. Depending on your state law, you might be in the uncomfortable position of "representing" both parties. Parties who are natural adversaries. Which means, by association, both parties now view you as an adversary too.

Negotiating your commission on a double-ended deal is something to discuss up front with your seller. Many savvy sellers will ask you at the time of listing if you will waive the buyer agent fee if you sell their home yourself. I always say no. They always seem surprised. Here's how I explain it to them.

"I sell real estate to earn a living. If I find a ready, willing and able buyer who is going to buy a home, I'd sure like to sell him a home and get paid for it. If I agree to reduce or waive the buyer agent commission if I bring the buyer to your home, that's a built-in incentive for me to take my buyers elsewhere. I think that's unethical. If I know that I'll make 3% for selling a buyer a house down the street, but only 1% if I sell him yours, it's going to be tempting for me to encourage him to buy the other house. And if I sell him your home, I'm doing the work of both agents, and it's only fair that I get paid for that."

I'm blunt this way; it's part of my charm. Some sellers like it, some don't. But it's my style. You will find your own. But my theory is absolutely above reproach. If you don't like my delivery, make up one that feels warm and fuzzy to you. But have an answer ready.

Now, truth be told, whenever I've double-ended a sale I have always kicked in part of my commission to make some problem go away. After all, being paid 5% or 6% on my listing is a pretty big paycheck and I'm motivated to make sure it closes.

Yet every time I've doubled-ended a sale, I've also said I'd never do it again. The money is sweet, but the sale itself is almost always ugly. Both sides are suspicious of you and your motives (perhaps with reason). Suddenly, the seller you promised your utmost loyalty to has to accept that you are assisting someone else to negotiate against him. He wonders what secrets he shared with you are now being shared with the buyer.

I double-ended my first listing. My sellers had told me early on that their bottom line was $155,000. Damned if my buyer didn't want to offer $155,000! My sellers came right out and accused me of disclosing their bottom line price to him and I can't blame them for wondering.

No matter how hard you try to be neutral, it's going to be difficult to 1) truly be neutral throughout the sale and 2) convince both parties that you are being neutral. Unless you're lucky and happen to put a cheerful seller and an easy-going buyer together, you're going to have some stressful moments.

A word of warning. If the buyer appears to be inexperienced, suspicious or otherwise difficult, I highly recommend referring him to another agent to represent him. As you gain experience, double-ending listings gets easier, but in the beginning, it's probably a good practice to protect yourself first.

Discounting Your Commission—the "Family" Discount

Here's a shocker. Your friends and family are going to assume you will give them a discount off your "standard" commission. Here's a bigger shocker. I say, do it!

It's the way of the world and you as a real estate agent are not so darn special that you don't have to participate. When you go have drinks at the bar where your buddy is bartending, don't you figure you'll get a drink on the house? If your best friend sells, let's say, vinyl windows, wouldn't you assume she'd get you a "great deal"? If your sister is an accountant, would you really expect to pay her full fee to do your taxes? So why do we real estate agents get so insulted and snotty when our close friends and family assume they'll get a great deal from their favorite real estate agent?

Don't worry, you won't be expected to, or even asked to cut everyone you know a "great deal." But don't be categorically opposed to the idea of commission discounting for special people. And making people feel special is a great way to generate good will and future referrals.

What about repeat customers and "frequent" buyers or sellers? Again, I have no problem making them feel special by reducing my fee for them. They are special and I can afford to cut my fee to keep them coming back.

your first lisitng

TURNING FOR SALE SIGNS TO SOLDS

Assuming you work in an office (as opposed to under your own steam) your office administrator will make darn sure you have all your paperwork complete. Corporate real estate offices tend to be pretty tight on such things, so I'll bet you'll get a checklist of the required contracts and disclosures. It's likely that your listing will not see the light of the MLS until everything is reviewed and found satisfactory by the paperwork Nazi—um, sorry, the office manager. No offense to office managers, someone has to keep us in line.

Following is my checklist, complete with my commentary, of the items I have found that need to be handled during the course of the listing, outside of the typical activities regulated and monitored by your office. This list has been developed and improved over years of selling real estate and is one of the most important tools I use in my real estate practice.

Checklist for New Listings

(You can find the checklist without my commentary, in the Appendix or at my website www.SellwithSoul.com)

THINGS TO DO PRIOR TO MLS ENTRY

✓ Get all contracts and disclosures completed and signed by seller

✓ Take pictures (see below)

THINGS TO DO THE DAY OF MLS ENTRY

✓ Schedule the virtual tour (see below)

✓ Get the key, install the lockbox

> *Make sure the key works smoothly in the lock! Don't make it hard for agents to get into the house. If your seller tells you there's a "trick" to unlocking the door, encourage the seller to have it repaired. No, insist on it.*

✓ Get the HOA contact information from seller

> *If applicable*

✓ Enter your listing on to the MLS

✓ Enter the listing in your contract manager program

> *If you use one*

✓ Order "Just Listed" cards

> *If your office pays for these, go ahead and order them. I do not recommend spending your own money on Just Listed/Just Sold cards, though.*

✓ Track the expiration date

> *When a listing expires, your seller is fair game for other agents to market to. It's terribly embarrassing to hear from your seller that real estate agents are prospecting him to let him know his listing expired. Make sure you have a system to alert you a week or two ahead of time. Your office manager probably tracks this for you, but confirm.*

✓ Install the For Sale sign

Be sure the placement of your sign complies with any city ordinances. In Denver, it's illegal to put a sign in the "tree lawn" which is the space between the sidewalk and the street. If you do put a sign there, it will be kidnapped by the sign police and held hostage.

✓ Give the seller's showing instructions to your office or showing service

✓ Create and display Special Feature cards in the home

Things like "New Air Conditioner!" "Don't Miss the Walk-in Closet!" "Don't let the cats out, please!" The more Special Features you can come up with, the more your seller will love you.

✓ Send a copy (e-mail or fax) of the MLS listing to seller for review

✓ Call the seller when his listing is activated

This is good PR and prepares him for showings.

THINGS TO DO RIGHT AFTER MLS ENTRY

✓ Deliver copies of all signed documents to your seller

✓ Prepare the home brochure (see below)—send to the printer

✓ Schedule the open house, put up OPEN SUNDAY rider on sign
If applicable

THINGS TO DO DURING THE FIRST WEEK OF YOUR LISTING

✓ Call the HOA and complete your questionnaire

If applicable; see Chapter Eight for details on the questionnaire.

✓ Pick up the home brochures, deliver to home

Don't put all the brochures in the outside box; if the lid is left open, your brochures can be ruined. Try to get your seller to help keep the box filled. If the home is vacant and you can't commit to keeping the box filled, take the brochure box down after your first batch of brochures are gone. Empty brochure boxes annoy buyers, which makes you look bad.

✓ Start providing showing feedback (see below)

✓ Load Internet advertising

✓ E-mail web links to seller (see below)

✓ Schedule Fluff & Flush visits
    If the home is vacant; see below for an explanation of "Fluffing & Flushing."

✓ Send first marketing package to seller (see below)

✓ Call seller, "Are the showing instructions working for you?" (see below)

THINGS TO DO THROUGHOUT THE LISTING PERIOD

✓ Call to check-in every ten days

✓ Fluff & flush every seven days
    If the home is vacant

✓ Check the status of home brochures every Thursday
    You want to make sure your brochure box is full for the weekend.

✓ Send market updates every three weeks

✓ Prepare and schedule your six-week CMA meeting

✓ Re-take your exterior photos
    If the seasons have changed, update your exterior photos. If it's June, a snowy MLS photo will scream "Desperate Seller Here!" to potential buyers and agents.

Your MLS Entry

Make your MLS entries accurate, clear and appealing. You don't need to list every single feature in the written description; your goal is to inspire agents and online buyers to schedule a showing.

Compare the following two listings:

> **2356 King Court**
> "Stng blk; lake shops dwntwn jst min away; updts inc newr mech syst, wd flrsundr crpt, nwr fxtrs in kitch/bath, tile kitch flrs, elc blnd, mechs drmovrsz 3 car gar (almst 1ksqft), imm poss."

Versus

> **4587 Queen Circle**
> "Total Remodel with a Twist! Loft Style! Exposed Brick! Exposed Ducts! New Hardwood Floors! New Maple Kitchen! New Granite Counters + Stainless Appliances! New Windows! Copper Gutters!"

Send a copy of the listing to your seller. This is critical. Your seller needs to acknowledge that everything is correct and accurate to the best of his knowledge. This protects both of you. Don't fret when he wants to "improve" your written description or asks why you didn't mention the custom dog door. Explain, as above, that the MLS description is designed to attract buyers and agents to the door; once inside the home, they will be wowed by all the additional special features. If he insists on adding more detail, go ahead and do it. This is not a battle worth fighting.

Photography and Virtual Tours

Digital photos are a must in today's world. Many buyers shop online for homes and will skip over a home that doesn't have interior pictures. Buy a quality camera with a wide-angle lens and a flash and learn to take good interior pictures.

JENNIFER'S $0.02...

Bad MLS photos are an embarrassment to our profession. If you want to see some examples of abysmally bad photos, go to Active Rain (www.activerain. com) and do a search for the phrase "bad MLS photos." Of course, you can probably find plenty of examples in your own MLS. It's almost comical, if it weren't so pathetic.

Virtual tours are not mandatory and if your seller doesn't request one, don't worry about it. A virtual tour (or lack thereof) probably won't affect the marketability of your listing. But if your seller wants one or you wish to include virtual tours in your listing services package, shop around for a good provider.

I do my own virtual tours. Managing your own tours has many advantages, but if you prefer to hire an outside company to do them for you, make sure to schedule the tour right away.

Home Brochures

Excerpted from
Your Successful Real Estate Career by Ken Edwards [4]

Should you include the asking price of the property on your flyer that you place in a box in the front yard? OK, whom are you representing? Whose interests are you putting above everyone else? Who gave you the authority to put the sign in the front yard? Of course, the answer to 'all of the above' is the homeowner who listed the property with you. People interested in that house want to know the asking price and if it's not there, they could simply move on out of frustration and look elsewhere. Some training programs counsel not including the price on the brochure, which will require the prospect to call the agent. That means it's a good potential marketing tool for the agent (perhaps for other listings that might be in the buyer's price range), but does it best serve the listing client? I report, you decide. If I'm your supervising broker, you know the answer.

Showing Feedback

As soon as you've had your first showing, your sellers will be screaming for feedback! You need to have a system in place for obtaining the commentary from buyers and their agents. If your showing service doesn't provide this service, or if you don't use a showing service, you can call or email agents yourself. There are also online companies who will do this for you.

---

4   Kenneth Edwards, Your Successful Real Estate Career,
     AMACOM, 2007, page 83

Market Updates

I send written communication to my seller every three weeks or so. The first package goes out in the first week and includes the full MLS printout and a list of the current competition for their home, with photos. In this first package, I promise my sellers a market update in three weeks showing any new listings, price reductions, homes under contract and recent closings.

Subsequent market update packages include the recent market activity as well as the number of showings, virtual tour hits, Realtor.com hits and any other activity data I can track. Truthfully, most of my sellers never seem that interested in my market updates, but I send them anyway just to stay in touch.

After sending four market update packages, I usually ask my seller if she would like to continue receiving my updates. If she does, I keep sending them. If she says no, I do the updates on my own, just to keep up on the market in her neighborhood.

If, in the course of preparing your market updates, you see a new listing that is competing with your listing, you should preview it right away. It will make a Very Good impression on your seller if you call her to tell her all about the new listing on her block. If the new listing makes her listing look overpriced, well, you should share that information with her too (or at least offer to show it to her).

Staying in Touch with Your Seller

One of the most common complaints of home sellers is that they never hear from the listing agent after the sign goes in the yard. And frankly, if there's not much going on, it is easy to let time go by without contact.

So I came up with several scheduled "topics" of discussion to give me an excuse to call my seller, even if I don't have much to report. For example, about a week into the listing, assuming we've had showings, I call my sellers to make sure the showing instructions are working for them or if they need to make adjustments. Other topics include my comments on any new competing listings I've previewed (see above), to check on their stash of flyers or to pass on feedback, of course. If my listing is vacant, I always call my seller after I go Fluffing & Flushing (see below) to report on the condition of the home. If there is anything he needs to address, or anything I corrected for him, I let him know.

Right after his home is listed, I send my seller an e-mail with all the links to the websites where his home is featured. I also include a link to the virtual tour and ask him to send the link out to his friends in hopes that someone will be interested. If nothing else, it's good advertising for me.

Six-Week Meeting with Seller

I tell my sellers up front that we will need to reevaluate the market about six weeks after we go on the market. Schedule an appointment with your sellers, prepare an updated CMA, review your feedback and show up with a plan and a smile.

Fluffing & Flushing

Fluffing & Flushing is the act of checking on a vacant listing during the listing period to ensure that everything is as it should be. And it never is. "Fluffing" refers to a general tidying up of the home (more below) and "Flushing"—well, have you noticed what happens to a toilet that hasn't been used in a while? Or worse—has been used but not flushed? Part of my service provided to my clients who own vacant homes is to flush their toilets for them!

If you have a vacant listing, you'll be dismayed how quickly things deteriorate into chaos. Shower curtains fall down, light bulbs burn out with incredible frequency, windows leak, lockboxes jam. Sure, it may be the seller's responsibility to maintain the showing readiness of their home, but if the home is vacant they won't—and if you want it to sell, you'll probably need to do it yourself.

If you find yourself with a lot of vacant listings, you'll want to pack a little crate for your car with the following items:

> Light bulbs
> Trash bags
> Dusting cloths
> Dirt Devil
> Windex and paper towels

I recommend checking on your vacant listings once a week. Here's what you're looking for:

Sign still up? Brochure box full? Lockbox operating smoothly? Porch light on? Yard need mowing? Watering? Snow being shoveled? Paper delivery canceled? Any strange smells in house? Power on? Heat on? Floor reasonably clean? Dead bugs? All doors locked? Windows secure? Toilets flushed? Garage door closed?

Gather up agent cards, flush the toilets, check the mailbox, make any corrections you can and make a note of conditions your seller needs to address. If nothing else, your weekly Fluff & Flush visits will give you something to talk to your seller about and show that you care!

Open Sunday!

As a new agent, you'll probably be happy to hold your listings open. A good open house with a lot of traffic is actually a lot of fun, but a dead open house—ugh—is deadly. But even if it doesn't sell the home, there are several good reasons to hold an open house:

- It makes your seller happy.

- If the open house is active, you can get a concentrated dose of feedback from the general public.

- Your open house may be the first time you've spent any real quality time in the home, so you may notice features or even potential problems that escaped your attention before.

- And of course, the real reason agents hold open houses—the opportunity to prospect for buyers.

However, as we discussed in Chapter Seven, don't forget that in your seller's eyes you are there to sell that home, not to prospect for buyers.

Once I showed up at an open house with color printouts from the MLS of other comparable homes for sale. Of course, I was planning to share these printouts with interested visitors to demonstrate my expertise in the market, as well as my willingness to show and sell other homes besides the one I was holding open.

The seller saw my printouts and was horrified. It had never occurred to her that I wasn't there solely for her benefit, and frankly, it hadn't occurred to me that this might bother her. But of course it did. Right or wrong, sellers put a lot of stock in your open house and they truly expect the offers to be rolling in by 4:05 p.m.

Home Staging

Real estate home staging is all the rage! With good reason...staging sells houses. I stage all my own personal properties before putting them on the market. If there is a home staging company in your town, find out what they do and roughly how much they charge. Some simply consult with your sellers and give them a list of projects to complete after the stager goes home. The better ones work with the homeowner to identify problem areas and help them make the improvements, using either the homeowner's own furniture and decorative items, or their own.

In my opinion, if a homeowner is talented enough to follow the designer's recommendations, he or she probably doesn't need to hire a home stager in the first place. I don't have the patience or skill to follow a stager's recommendations. My favorite staging company is turn-key. The designer shows up at the home for a consultation and comes back the next day ready to move furniture! The results are nothing short of amazing. Check out www.StagingDenver.com for a great description of home staging and some fun before and after photos.

Who pays? Well, either you or the seller or both. If your market is booming and it's a sure thing that your listing will sell, you might consider offering staging as an incentive to hire you. After all, if the market is that darn good, listings are money in the bank! I used to pay to stage all my vacant listings until the market unexpectedly plummeted (without warning me!). Unfortunately at that time I had 27 listings, many of them staged, none under contract...ouch. But I digress. If you're a believer in the power of a staged home, you won't have any trouble persuading your sellers to hire a stager and pay for it.

One caveat...Never ever stage a home that needs work. Oh yes, you'll "sell it"... over and over again. The buyer for a staged home is typically not Jane Handy woman, willing to overlook minor imperfections or deferred maintenance. She'll fall in love with the home, then run screaming from it after the inspection. As a corollary, don't stage a home to hide material defects. To improve the perceived livability of difficult space? YES! To hide a structural crack in the bedroom? Nooooo.

SELLING YOUR LISTING

Negotiating Offers

It's terribly exciting when you get offers on your first few listings. Well, actually, it's always exciting, even on your 90th listing.

When the offer(s) come in, your sellers will look to you for guidance. Hopefully.

Offers come in all shapes and sizes, with any combination of both attractive and deal-breaking provisions. Maybe the price is good, but the closing date is too far out. Or the price is low, but there's no inspection contingency. Rarely are offers everything you hope they'll be. Even in a multiple offer situation, there is often no clear winner—every offer has its quirks.

Here are the four most likely offer scenarios:

Good Offers

As you can imagine, these are the most fun and the easiest to negotiate. Obviously, a "good" offer is full price or close to, meets the seller's needs for timing and proposes reasonable dates and deadlines.

However, as the listing agent, I almost always look for something to counter in every offer. Even if the offer is close to perfect, I don't like to have my seller sign an offer as written. I have several reasons for this strategy.

First, I believe that if a buyer is going to have buyer's remorse, I'd rather get that over with up front. By countering the offer, even on a technicality, it gives the buyer an out if she is wavering. Some agents vehemently disagree with this strategy—they want that deal executed now. But since most contracts have inspection and loan contingencies, the buyer can easily terminate the contract after it is executed. And it's far more painful to terminate a deal than to never put it together in the first place.

Second, countering an offer keeps the balance of power ever so slightly tilted toward the seller (your client!). Yes, he is excited to receive such a fine offer on his house, but he's not desperate.

Third, when her offer is accepted as written, the buyer may wonder if she got her best deal. She begins to question herself, setting the stage for buyer's remorse. Maybe she should have offered less? By introducing a counterproposal, even if it isn't related to price, both buyer and seller feel the "thrill" of a successful negotiation.

Low Offers

Everyone wants a deal. Many buyers want to try a lowball offer to see what happens. If your seller acts offended, go ahead and be offended with him. You'll win brownie points for being on his team. If you defend the low offer, he'll wonder if maybe you're in cahoots with the buyer's agent. Yes, sellers do think this way.

Once the seller has blown off a little steam (with your help!) and the annoyance is out of his system, you can begin to calmly discuss your counterproposal. Ensure that your seller is clear about the other provisions of the offer (besides price) such as the inspection period, the closing date, the date of possession and any requested seller-paid closing costs. Be sure to check your listing agreement ahead of time to refresh your memory on any exclusions! Point out the requested inclusions (e.g., refrigerator, washer, dryer, etc.) to the seller to make sure the buyer agent didn't sneak something in on you that your seller meant to exclude. I recently got to buy a washer and dryer for a seller because the buyer asked for them in the contract and the seller had specifically excluded them. And I forgot.

Your seller may want to counter at full price just to make a statement of his displeasure with the low offer. Try to get him to give a little bit (maybe a few thousand dollars), which will allow the buyer to accept without looking like a total putz. But if your seller is adamant, go ahead and cheerfully follow his direction. He is the boss!

What if your listing is overpriced and the low offer is reasonable? Well, hopefully your seller is aware that you think the price is high and that he pushed you to "give it a try." If that's the case, the best thing to do is to matter-of-factly remind the seller that buyer agents are looking at the same data you looked at when you gave your pricing recommendation. Period. Don't look smug or frustrated. Your seller isn't stupid and he needs to feel your support in order to make the right decision.

You'll put these deals together more often than you might think. Even a dismal offer can often be successfully negotiated.

Multiple Offers

If you are in a market where multiple offers are common, your broker can probably better advise you on the local nuances of multiple-offer negotiation. Different states have different laws regarding the proper way to respond. I will tell you how I did it in Colorado, but be sure to check with your broker to make sure these strategies are legal and acceptable in your market.

Be sure that all buyer agents know that a bidding war is brewing. This can only help your seller get a higher price. Don't let anyone tell you that encouraging a bidding war is unethical. Nonsense!

> If there is no clear winner among the offers (i.e., they are all strong), you can do one of two things:
>
> 1. You can notify all buyer agents that their buyer should present their best offer by a specific deadline (e.g., 6 p.m.). Tell them all offers will be presented at that time.
>
> 2. Counter all offers with an appropriate disclosure stating that there are multiple counterproposals in circulation (ask your broker for a sample).

Be aware that a bidding war may result in some conflicting emotions for both the seller and the winning buyer. The seller may feel an inflated sense of power over the buyer (and the market) and refuse to be reasonable during the inspection period and any subsequent negotiations. The buyer, on the other hand, may feel a little buyer's remorse after all the excitement and wonder if she got carried away in the bidding process. She may feel that the home better darn well be perfect and she may be overly fussy at the inspection.

Contingent Offers

A contingent offer is one in which the buyer needs to sell a home to qualify to buy your listing. Here are three responses to a contingent offer:

> 1. Reject it, who needs the hassle?

2. Accept it, hopefully the buyer will be able to sell his home.

3. Counter with a First Right of Refusal.

Countering the offer with a First Right of Refusal means that the seller accepts the offer, but will continue to market the property. If the seller receives another acceptable offer, the seller notifies the first buyer that he must remove his home-sale contingency (and prove that he can close without selling his current home). If the buyer cannot or will not remove his contingency, then that contract is terminated and the seller is free to accept the second offer.

Contracts with home sale contingencies are full of problems. Even if the contingent buyer is able to find a buyer for his home, the likelihood of your listing closing with this buyer is about half what it is with a typical non-contingent buyer. Think about it, instead of one potential deal-breaking inspection, there are two (the one on your listing and the one on the buyer's home). Instead of one loan approval contingency, there are two. Not one appraisal, two. Twice the opportunity for buyer's remorse or an unexpected job relocation.

So why would you ever accept a contingency? A few reasons:

More Money

A good buyer agent knows that a contract contingent upon a home sale is not as appealing as a clean contract, therefore, the offer should be as attractive as possible in other respects. If you receive a contingent offer, you should expect a great price and reasonable terms.

Market Realities

As real estate prices move higher, first-time buyers are finding it harder to purchase a home. Therefore, the buyer for your listing may already be a homeowner who needs to sell his home to qualify to buy a new home.

In general, if your seller is committed to a specific moving date, it is probably a good idea to avoid contingent offers. Although, as discouraging as all this may sound, in my experience, most contingent deals do close. They're complicated and time consuming, but if everyone can stay cool and flexible, there's a good chance of success!

Closing Your Listing

Incidentally, the seeds of this book were planted way back in my rookie year when I put my first listing under contract. I proudly marched into my office, with my executed contract and earnest money in hand ready to turn over to the office manager. She congratulated me and then asked which title company I was going to use. Huh?

Not wanting to appear clueless, I mumbled a non-answer and hurried away before she could push me for more details. I realized that I was experiencing one of those "you don't know what you don't know" moments. I surreptitiously asked the more experienced agents if I could borrow their "listing checklist"— y'know, the list they were given in real estate training to guide them through the contract-to-closing period? I must have missed that class because I never got mine. A Twilight Zone moment (for me). No one knew of such a list.

> **TITLE WORK**
>
> *As used in this book, title work is the documentation provided by the title company showing current ownership of a property, along with any liens recorded against the property. In Colorado, "title work" also includes recorded HOA documents such as covenants and condominium declarations.*

Some things I didn't know were my responsibility:

- Choosing the title company and ordering title work
- Preparing for and attending the appraisal
- Bringing the earnest money to closing
- Making sure all the disclosures are signed by the buyer
- Bringing the house key to the closing
- Taking down the sign and retrieving my lockbox and brochure box

Sure, I knew these things happened, I just didn't realize I was the one who was supposed to make them happen...

Somehow I muddled through and got the house closed. I promised myself that I would create a checklist for myself with all the details that need to be handled as the listing agent during the contract-to-closing period. And thus—a checklist queen was born.

Handling Inspections...
as the Listing/Seller's Agent

JENNIFER'S $0.02...

Subtly ask your seller to vacate the home during the inspection. The buyers need to start mentally taking possession of the home and this can't happen if the seller is hovering over them. Inspections are stressful, and the fewer personalities in the mix, the better.

As the listing agent, your primary job is to keep your seller calm during the inspection process. You'll also help him determine the best response to the buyer's demands, one that feels fair to him (or nearly so), yet satisfies the buyer. You may have to help him obtain bids for the requested corrections and/or coordinate repairs.

A new listing agent can feel helpless when presented with a laundry list of inspection requests. Typically, she gives it to her client (the home seller), asks what the client would like to do, and passively delivers the response to the buyer's agent. The response is either acceptable or it's not, either way, the seller's agent (you) did not take control and "solve the problem."

Remember, sellers hire you to sell their house and get them to a closing. Believe it or not, they may not want to discuss or have an opinion on every single issue. If you appear to be in control of the situation, they will usually take your advice.

Of course, you need to know what to advise—especially during the inspection period. Every inspection negotiation is unique. Some sellers are sympathetic to the emotions and fears of the homebuyer; some think their home is perfect and are insulted by any insinuations to the contrary. Some have discretionary funds to make laundry list repairs; some are wondering if they will have enough equity to come to closing without their checkbook. I'll address each scenario below.

The Perfect Seller

This seller understands that his home isn't perfect and that agreeing to reasonable inspection requests is just a part of the home-selling process. He is probably rather handy and is happy (well, not unhappy) to make most of the repairs requested by the buyer. Even silly ones. You will have sellers like this, but as you can expect, not often. It's usually cheaper for the handy seller to make the nickel-and-dime repairs than for him to negotiate a credit with the buyer, so that's what I usually encourage him to do.

The Easily Offended Seller

This seller doesn't want to fix anything. She has been difficult since Day One, and might not want your advice anyway. She'll make comments like, "It was like that when we bought the house" or "There's nothing wrong with the furnace, it works fine," even though the inspector's report indicates a carbon monoxide leak. When you are working with these sellers, here are a few strategies to get you past the inspection period.

Try to negotiate a dollar amount your seller is willing to spend toward repairs in the original contract. For example, you could state in your counterproposal, "Seller shall pay no more than $500 toward inspection items." This puts the buyer on notice that the seller will not be nickel and dime'd and, while it's not fool-proof, it works more often than you would expect. Some states already incorporate this wording into their contracts; perhaps yours does.

Sometimes if you say to your seller, "When you buy your next home, will you expect the major systems to be in good working order and if they aren't, will you expect the seller to fix them?" This works especially well if you will also be the buyer agent for the seller's replacement home. Or say (very casually), "If I were the buyer's agent, I probably would ask for these items too."

On the other hand, remember whom you represent. If your seller does not want to fix anything and she thinks she is being reasonable, make your case once and then shut up. For two reasons. First, you never know, the buyer might just back down and accept the home "as is" and if you tried to pressure your seller into doing more (and lost), you will look Very Bad in your seller's eyes. She will think you were trying to spend her money in order to secure your commission.

Second, if the deal crashes over the inspection, the seller has a bigger problem than you do (you hope). Yes, I realize you just watched your paycheck vanish before your eyes, but hopefully your seller learned that you do know what you're talking about. Maybe she'll even look into the price of replacing that 60- year-old furnace she is so proud of.

I have worked with sellers who were so unreasonable at inspection that I had to terminate the listing because they clearly did not have a strong enough need to sell their home. But not often.

The Cash Poor Seller

If your seller has equity in his home, but no cash on hand, inspection issues can be easily solved. You have two options. The safest thing to do in this situation is to negotiate a credit for the repairs that is paid at closing so that the buyer can make the repairs himself afterward. This credit will be taken from the seller's proceeds. If the buyer insists that the seller complete the repairs prior to closing, try to schedule the repairs as close to the closing date as possible so that the chances of buyer default are minimal. Arrange for the contractors to be paid at closing, again, out of the proceeds of the sale. Of course, if the sale unexpectedly fails, the seller will be liable for the repairs and you need to ensure he understands this risk.

If your seller has neither the funds nor the equity to make repairs, he simply may not be able to sell his home at this time. His needs and desires are irrelevant to the needs and desires of the market and he shouldn't expect a buyer to be sympathetic to his financial troubles. If the needed repairs are relatively minor and/or cosmetic, you might be able to persuade the buyer (or their agent) to accept the home "as is," but a good buyer agent will negotiate a lower sales price. So your seller still loses.

A smart listing agent points out areas of concern (older furnace, worn roof, cracked windows, etc.) to the seller prior to listing. Don't dwell on these issues, just comment on them and gauge the seller's response. If he argues vehemently with you (and most will), just smile sweetly and say something like, "Okay, no problem," then move on to other topics. And know that inspection will likely be a struggle.

On the other hand, don't be afraid to advise your seller to say "no" to the buyer's requests if they are truly unreasonable. But if your seller wants to sell and the buyer wants to buy, even difficult inspections can usually be successfully negotiated.

The Appraisal

The appraisal is a justification of value. Appraisals are done by a professional appraiser hired by the lender or bank that the buyer is using for his mortgage to purchase your listing. As long as the appraiser values the property at the negotiated sales price or higher, there is no problem, mon. If it comes in lower, big problem, my friend.

Here is how the appraisal process works:

1. The lender or bank contacts the appraiser and assigns him the appraisal on your listing.

2. The appraiser contacts you (the listing agent) to gain access to the home.

3. The appraiser physically inspects the home, measures the interior and exterior, notes the features (bedrooms, baths, updating, amenities, etc.) and take photos.

4. The appraiser analyzes the data and determines the market value.

5. The appraiser communicates the market value to the lender and provides a full report, which will be reviewed by the lender's underwriter prior to loan approval.

As the listing agent, you have several responsibilities. First, I always recommend that listing agents meet the appraiser at the property for the appraisal. Frankly, I think appraisers would prefer that we don't, but I feel it is our responsibility to show up anyway (just stay out of his way and don't take up his time with small-talk, unless he initiates it). Being at the appraisal is the professional thing to do and your seller will appreciate your presence there. And, if a problem arises with value and you weren't there...? The seller will wonder if you were negligent. I'm not particularly suspicious, but I feel it is good karma to be at an appraisal—more than once, an appraisal "problem" arose over an appraisal that I didn't attend.

Second, you need to be prepared for the appraisal with a written list of all upgrades the seller has made to the property with the approximate cost of each. If the air conditioner is an upgraded model, list that. If the new wood floors are Brazilian cherry that cost twice as much as #2 red oak, make sure the appraiser knows it. If the window coverings are a special brand and custom -made, include them on your list.

Third, show the appraiser the sold comparables you used to price the home (assuming your comparables justify your sales price!) If there are reasonable comparables out there that might indicate a lower sales price, be prepared to explain to the appraiser why you didn't use them. For example, if the house across the street sold for $20,000 less than your listing, you need to know why and be able to explain this clearly to the appraiser. Perhaps it was an in-family sale, or maybe the house had a strong cat urine smell. Whatever the reason, the appraiser needs an explanation or he might be duty-bound to use that home as a comparable, which could threaten your sales price.

One thing to know about appraisers, and one great reason to be prepared ahead of time is that they hate to be hassled about market value after their appraisal is completed. Once they determine a market value, it's tough to talk them out of it. Is it ego? Maybe. Or perhaps it's just that they don't have time to argue with listing agents all over town who should have been prepared in the first place. So, make sure the appraiser has all the information he or she needs up-front and don't depend on having the opportunity to defend your sales price after the appraisal is complete.

CHECKLIST FOR LISTINGS UNDER CONTRACT

This checklist addresses the items that are your responsibility during the period from contract-to-closing, as the listing agent. You can find the checklist without my commentary in the Appendix and on my website. It is formatted to be used as a check-off sheet for each listing if you aren't yet using a contract management program.

THINGS TO DO RIGHT AFTER CONTRACT IS EXECUTED

✓ Get the earnest money check
> *If the offer and subsequent negotiations were handled via fax, don't forget to get the earnest money!*

✓ Turn in the executed contract to your office manager

✓ Put contract dates in your contract manager program if you use one
> *Important dates include any objection deadlines (inspection, insurance, title, covenant review, appraisal, etc.), loan approval or any other agreements made in the contract. If you don't use a contract management program, enter these dates in your planner.*

✓ Order the title work (if it's your job to do so; each state is different)

✓ Order HOA documents, if applicable
> *If your contract calls for the seller to provide recent HOA financial statements and/or meeting minutes, get these ordered right away if your seller doesn't have them (they never do). Some HOA managers now charge to provide this information, FYI.*

✓ Change the contract status in the MLS

✓ Notify any agents with pending showings of the status change

✓ Send the disclosures to the buyer's agent

✓ Call the buyer's lender to introduce yourself

THINGS TO DO THE FIRST WEEK AFTER CONTRACT

✓ Pick up the brochure box

✓ Get payoff information from your seller
To pay off the seller's current loan, the title company will need the seller's social security number(s) and the seller's lender information (account number, customer service phone number). Don't forget to get this information for any second mortgages or home equity loans.

✓ Has the buyer signed and returned the disclosures?

✓ Put up SOLD sign

✓ Call the buyer's lender to check on loan progress

THINGS TO DO TWO WEEKS AFTER CONTRACT

✓ Prepare for the appraisal
As the listing agent, you should attend the appraisal with your sold comparables in hand, ready to defend the sales price if necessary. You should also have a printed list of all the upgrades and improvements to give the appraiser. Even if you have no reason to worry about the appraisal, it's a good idea to meet the appraiser at the property. It's professional and makes a good impression on your seller.

✓ Set the closing
Notify all parties (seller, buyer agent, lender) of the time, date and location of closing.

THINGS TO DO DURING THE WEEK BEFORE CLOSING

✓ Confirm that the inspection items are complete or scheduled

✓ Confirm that the seller has arranged a move out cleaning
More than once I have personally cleaned one of my listings because the seller didn't do it. It's embarrassing and awkward

(and I'm a terrible maid). Now, I always ask my seller if she has arranged to have the home cleaned or if she needs me to arrange it. At least it puts her on notice that the buyer is expecting the home to be delivered in maid-clean condition.

✓ Arrange a mail-out close or Power of Attorney (POA) if necessary
If your seller can't attend closing, make sure the title company knows ahead of time. They will send the closing package to the seller or prepare a POA for someone else to sign the closing documents.

✓ Are there any changes that need to be communicated to the lender or title company?
Many times, contract provisions will be changed or renegotiated and no one remembers to let the lender and/or title company know. If you surprise the lender or title company with a material change at the last minute, your closing may be delayed, which makes everyone sad...

✓ Is the buyer doing a walk-thru?
If so, let your seller know about it and leave the lockbox on the home. This is a good time to confirm with your seller that all the inspection items have been completed.

✓ Confirm the closing date, time and location with all parties

THINGS TO DO RIGHT BEFORE CLOSING

✓ Review the closing figures
Go over the figures with your seller to ensure there are no surprises at the closing table. If the seller's proceeds are different from the seller's expectations, now is the time to figure out why...not at the closing!

✓ Order earnest money from your office manager, if applicable
Check with your office manager to see how earnest money escrows are handled. Protocol varies widely here. Just find out if there's something you are supposed to do.

✓ Prepare the file for closing

✓ Pick up the sign, lockbox and interior brochure box

AFTER CLOSING

✓ Turn in the file to the office manager

✓ Update your seller's address in your SOI manager

✓ Call the seller a few days after move-out
  Just thank him for his business and let him know you are always available for any post-closing questions or problems that may arise.

✓ Add the seller to your post-closing follow-up plan

✓ Update your website(s) with the sale

■ ■ ■ ■ ■

serving your client, not your paycheck

ADVENTURES IN AGENCY & THE OPEN CHECKBOOK POLICY

Adventures in Agency

P robably one of the first classes you took in real estate school was about agency. Whom you represent and how you represent them in a real estate transaction. This seemingly simple concept can generate hours of debate, , even in advanced real estate classrooms. In every GRI class I took, we always spent at least an hour discussing agency issues, even in classes that had nothing to do with client representation.

Even experienced agents can forget the nature of their agency obligations. When you represent a client as his agent, you are obligated to look after his best interests and enabled to act on his behalf. Other interests shouldn't intrude—not yours, not the cooperating agent's, not the other party's (buyer or seller). In our enthusiastic negotiation, sometimes we lose sight of the party we are hired to protect, advise and be an advocate for. It happens.

This chapter is not meant to be a refresher course on the finer points of your market's agency laws and practices, or even an overview of the topic. You can find plenty of basic and continuing education opportunities to learn about agency and disclosure requirements, and it's a good idea to take one of these classes every so often—especially if you find yourself getting a little lax (it happens to all of us) in your own real estate practice.

Always keep your client's interests in the forefront of your mind and you won't go wrong. It's not always easy to do, because, believe me, even the most docile buyers or sellers are suspicious of you and will notice if you appear to place someone else's interests above theirs. Even if you are innocent, our profession has enough trust issues with the public; try not to add more. Just make sure you always strive to CYA by remembering who you are legally obligated to represent. (Hint, it's never you.)

Agency and Multiple Offers

Early in my career, which was during the Denver real estate boom, I put a 1923 Bungalow on the market on a Monday morning. The home had been renovated and professionally staged. At 6:00 p.m. I had one offer on the home. It was not a perfect offer—it was not full price and was contingent upon the sale of the buyer's home. By 9:00 p.m., I had three phone calls from other agents telling me they were also bringing me offers. I let these three agents know that there was an offer on the table, and that it appeared a bidding war was brewing.

My seller was pleased with these developments (this is not always the case if it occurs to your seller that you might have underpriced his home). He instructed me to gather all offers and to do whatever I needed to do to elicit the best offer from each. We scheduled a time to meet the following evening to review all the offers.

Meanwhile, the agent for offer #1 was getting annoyed with me. He accused me of generating a bidding war (uh, yeah), and eventually threatened me with a complaint to the local Board of Realtors®. As I recall, the term he used was "ethical midget." Being rather new in the business, I was intimidated by his antics and immediately questioned myself—was I violating some unwritten code of conduct between real estate agents? (To clarify, in Colorado, there is no "first come—first served" rule when offers are made. Sellers do not have to respond to offers in the order they come in—they may pick and choose among all presented and respond to whichever one appeals to them. Your state may have different requirements.)

We did indeed receive four offers on the home, one of which my seller accepted as written. It was an over-full-price, non-contingent offer with a three-week closing. The troublesome agent for the first offer harassed me for a week or so, but to my knowledge never took it any further. But his contention that I was unethical for encouraging a bidding war was way off base. My job was not to help him make his buyer happy, unfortunately. It's too bad that his buyer didn't win, but she wasn't the highest bidder. My job was to get my client (the seller) the most money and best terms for his home. Which I did.

I took an ethics class once where the instructor came right out and said, "Agents should always be on the lookout for opportunities to make allies among other agents." He used a multiple-offer situation, similar to the one above, to illustrate how we can "do the right thing" to our fellow real estate professionals and thus guarantee smoother transactions on future encounters with these other agents. His recommendation when a bidding war is looming is to always try to work with the first offer you receive to "honor" that buyer and agent. That the agent will always remember and appreciate that you nipped a bidding war in the bud, just for him. Helloooooooo? If you cost your seller $10,000 because you refuse to generate a bidding war, do you think your seller will be sympathetic to your need for Friends in the Business on your Future Deals?

Agency and Open Houses

Open houses are an area of much confusion when it comes to agency representation. I'm sure you have been taught what a great prospecting opportunity an open house can be—entire classes are taught on how to pick up buyers and solicit neighbors for future listings. However, please don't ever lose sight of why you're there.

Your job is to sell that home. If a potential buyer visits your open house and announces that she already has a buyer agent (who is probably taking the day off), you still need to graciously market the home to her. Show her around, politely answer her questions and, if you sense real interest, don't fuss that you're "wasting your time" on someone who isn't going to become your client.

Agency and Represented Buyers

If you have a lot of listings, you will find yourself doing the work of buyer agents who are apparently too darn lazy to actually show homes to their buyers. When I sold real estate full-time, I got at least one phone call a week from a buyer who had an agent, but didn't want to "bother him" until he found the house on his own. So, Mr. Buyer called listing agents all over town instead. Yes, it's your job to show your listing to this guy. If you refuse to show your listing to represented buyers, you could get in trouble with your seller, who expects you to show his home to any qualified buyer who calls.

I had a $900,000 listing once. My area of expertise at the time was in the $200,000 to $400,000 range, so this was a Big Deal to me. I was amazed how many potential buyers called me directly, bypassing their buyer agents because "they didn't want to bother him, he's so busy." Of course, the buyer agents would expect to be paid a hefty commission ($25,000!) if their buyers bought the home, but they were just so darn busy <sigh>.

So, I showed the home and showed the home and showed the home, mostly to represented buyers. It was my job and I didn't even complain too much about it. Again, many listing agents will refuse to show their listing to buyers who have agents, and this is just plain wrong. Like it or not, it is your job to market your listing to all interested buyers, which in my opinion, includes showing it to buyers who already have a buyer agent.

However, one buyer took it a step further and pushed me over my limit. I showed the home to him three times, and then he asked me to "draft up a contract" for his agent's review because his agent was getting ready to go on vacation and didn't have time. What would you do?

Unfortunately, I told the buyer to get his agent involved and earn his commission. And I got fired from the listing for it, rightly so. My job was to sell that house. It wasn't my seller's problem that the buyer's agent was lazy. The seller wanted a closing, and he didn't care how resentful I might be paying the other agent who did next to nothing. I should have continued to work with the buyer (with the proper disclosures of course), keeping his enthusiasm high, and increasing his commitment level. Unfortunately, when the buyer's agent finally showed up, he talked the buyer out of the home—and I got fired.

Even knowing the outcome, if I had it to do all over again, I'm not sure if I could have handled the situation any differently. Some scenarios don't have a black and white answer, and if you can't handle that, you are in the wrong business. Just realize that there are jerks in real estate, just as in any other business. Even by being technically correct, you will get burned, you will get fired, you will get, pardon my French, screwed. It's an unfortunate part of the game and you must accept it.

I came up with one semi-effective way to tactfully encourage buyers to "bother" their agents. When they tell me they have an agent, I ask them to contact their agent and let the agent know that I am showing the property to them. I tell the buyer it's because most buyer agents would much prefer to show their clients homes personally (one would hope), and get annoyed with listing agents who don't refer the buyer back to their buyer agent. Sometimes it works; most of the time, I just get to do the buyer agent's work for him. Ah well, all in a day's work.

John and the Dangerous Furnace

During the first semester of my rookie year, I worked with a buyer named John. The inspection on John's house revealed a dangerous furnace, emitting high levels of carbon monoxide. Since the home was occupied by a family with three small children, I notified the listing agent right away and asked in my inspection notice that the furnace be evaluated and replaced if necessary. The listing agent said, and I quote, "There's nothing wrong with that furnace and I would be happy to put that in writing for you! I should have known better than to accept an offer from a new agent, you obviously don't know what you're doing."

Huh?

But apparently he relayed the information to his sellers, who had a slightly different approach. They had the furnace checked out and confirmed that it was indeed dangerous and that the family could die in their sleep some night. The listing agent called me up all chipper and cheerful with the news and casually asked me to call my buyer to see if he "wanted to pay half of the replacement cost of a new furnace."

Without analyzing the situation, I called up John and brought him up to date, including the seller's "offer" that John contribute to the replacement. John was quiet for a minute, then asked me innocently enough, "And why would I want to do that?"

Duh.

Why indeed? I stumbled around for an answer, couldn't find one. My inexperience led me to try to please the listing agent and seller instead of properly advising my client, the buyer. No major harm done, except that I looked a little foolish; we refused to contribute toward the cost of the new furnace and moved on to closing.

You may be saying to yourself that you would never do something so brainless, and I hope you're right. But in the heat of negotiation, especially a contentious one, you might find yourself bending over backwards—in the wrong direction.

THE OPEN CHECKBOOK POLICY

When I was in real estate school, the instructor gave us a scenario that went something like this..."You are in the heat of negotiations for a buyer client. You're close, but the buyer and seller are arguing over the possession of the refrigerator. It doesn't appear that either side is going to give and you're watching your paycheck vanish before your eyes over a crummy used appliance. The thought of hitting the streets again with this buyer makes your heart sink. Your buyer is not going to buy this home unless he gets a refrigerator—it's a matter of pride now. What do you do?"

We Licensees-in-Training were stumped. We threw out some suggestions; mostly along the lines of convincing either buyer or seller to change their mind. Nope, not what our instructor was looking for.

"You can buy the refrigerator" was his solution.

We were horrified. Not one of us had considered that possibility. Most of us came from traditional W-2 employment situations and were not yet in tune with the realities of self-employment...i.e., you do what you gotta do to secure your paycheck. It was a huge Ah ha moment and 11 years later I still haven't forgotten it.

There will be times during your real estate career—and not just in the beginning—when opening your checkbook to make a problem go away is just good sense. Sometimes the problem at hand is actually your fault <gasp>. Sometimes it's just due to factors beyond your control and it may be the least painful way to get you to the closing. As you get more experienced and you learn to troubleshoot, hopefully these "opportunities" will present themselves less frequently. In the meantime, just consider these checks to be a cost of doing business and, more importantly, a learning experience. Tired of that phrase yet?

I'm the Proud Owner of a...Dead Tree!

My third sale ever, in November (which is relevant), my buyer client put a small home under contract on the east side of Denver. It was a rather stressful transaction, but it did close.

The following summer, my client called me, furious about a huge dead tree in his front yard. He insisted that the seller hadn't disclosed the existence of the dead tree, and it was going to cost him at least $1,000 to have it removed. I vaguely remembered seeing something about a "dead or diseased tree" in the Seller's Property Disclosure, and confidently went to the file to pull it out. "Ah ha!" I exclaimed to myself, "Here it is!" And, indeed, there it was, plain as day—the sellers did disclose the existence of a dead tree. I was relieved that I wasn't going to have to make an issue about non-disclosure.

But...uh oh.

My buyer hadn't signed the disclosure. No initials, no signature, no evidence that he ever even saw it. So there I was—no proof that I had ever presented the Seller's Property Disclosure to my client.

I wrote my buyer a check for $1,000. I did it cheerfully, without argument. It was my fault—I was his buyer agent. Sure, it was a painful check to write during my business-building period, but I did it. And, you know what? He still refers people to me and still fondly remembers that I bought his dead tree. It's turned into a good story and bought me more good PR than all the feel-good mailers in the world could have.

Don't be too proud to take responsibility for your mistakes. You'll be surprised at the good press you will receive for your integrity (not to mention the soul satisfaction).

HAVE YOU GONE BEYOND THE CALL OF DUTY LATELY?
by Bryant Tutas

Bought a new stove today. Unfortunately it won't be coming to my house but will be delivered to the house I closed on last week. The Sellers, my customers, were supposed to put a new stove in the house but decided to cut corners and put in a refurbished stove instead. Looks great. Works great. But it's not new. Neither the Buyers nor their Realtor did a walk through prior to closing and I didn't notice it when I was in the house. The Sellers are going through a nasty divorce and had already moved and gone their separate ways.

So what are you going to do? The Buyers are expecting a new stove when they arrive next week. I figure my Sellers have enough on their plate and I know that calling them on this is just going to create more tension between them. So I bought a new stove. Haven't seen it but hear it is really nice. Real shiny. Think I'll place a few business card magnets on the front and write the Buyers a little letter letting them know how I solved this problem for them. Maybe I'll get some business from it in the future. Maybe they will invite me over to dinner since my lovely wife doesn't cook.

Have you gone beyond the call of duty lately?

This One Hurt

My fix-n-flip clients, Barbie and Ken, purchased a crummy little house on a crummy little street—can you tell I was less than enthusiastic about their purchase? I hated the house and wasn't excited about the prospect of selling it for them down the line after they renovated it. I didn't think it was marketable and knew they would eventually blame me when the home didn't sell.

The home was an 1890 cracker box (sorry, single story home) with a finished attic. The attic area had sloping ceilings, which made it usable only for children or small adults. The access stairs were steep and difficult.

Miracles do happen and we found a buyer for the home. All was going well until the appraisal. The appraiser refused to consider the attic space in his total square footage, due to the sloped ceilings and difficult stairway, and reduced the value of the home accordingly; I believe he appraised the home $10,000 lower than the sales price.

My sellers were furious...at me. It hadn't occurred to me that the attic space might be an appraisal problem, although I had certainly been concerned about it as a marketing challenge. Barbie and Ken claimed I should have warned them about a potential appraisal problem before they purchased the property and perhaps they were right. But regardless, my sellers were going to have to reduce their sales price by $10,000 if they wanted a closing. I (grudgingly this time) kicked in my entire commission on the home to help offset their loss.

Oops! The HOA Fees Went Up!

When you're working with condos and townhomes (see Chapter Twelve), you need to be aware of a whole new set of issues. One of these is the changing Home Owners Association (HOA) fees. HOA's can and do raise their fees. If you are listing a property with an HOA, you need to periodically check in with your seller or the HOA itself to confirm that the fee you are advertising is still correct. If your buyer is purchasing a property with an HOA, you or your buyer should call the HOA directly to confirm the fee.

I once represented a buyer in the purchase of a $50,000 condo. The condo had been on the market for six months and the HOA fee advertised in the listing material was $150/month. At the closing, we discovered that the fee was actually $175/month. Either the listing agent made a mistake or the fee had been increased during the term of the listing, but either way, my buyer wasn't happy at all.

Increasing the monthly payment on a $50,000 condo by $25 is a Big Deal to the buyer of a $50,000 condo. Not just out of principle; it was truly a financial burden for her. After an awkward pause, I offered to reimburse my buyer one year's worth of the difference (25 X 12 = $300). I fully expected the listing agent to kick in too since it was clearly his misadvertising, but he did not. Technically, as a buyer agent, it was probably my responsibility to protect my buyer, but I did feel that the listing agent could have shown a little soul and kicked in a couple of dollars.

Kathy's Stove

Even if you have been selling real estate for 50 years, you will still come across situations that you couldn't have anticipated. The kind that will make you look like the bad guy if you don't fix them for your client. Which will often involve a check with your signature on it.

I sold a condo to my buyer, Kathy. Kathy was scraping her pennies together for the down payment and closing costs and didn't have much left over. During the inspection of the condo, we discovered that the stove didn't work and asked the seller to replace the stove with a comparable unit (thought I covered myself there!). The seller agreed and we proceeded toward closing.

The day of the final walk-thru just prior to closing, we discovered that the stove the seller purchased didn't fit into the space where the stove was supposed to go. It was too big (huh?)...apparently the stove that had been in the condo was the original stove put in by the builder and was a custom size (probably due to an expensive mistake by the kitchen designer). The replacement stove purchased by the seller protruded from the front of the cabinets about four inches, and blocked the dishwasher and a drawer from opening. Gee, I didn't think to put in my inspection notice that the stove should fit!

CAUTION!

Beware of homes with freshly renovated kitchens! The space allowed for appliances is not always standard, especially the space for the refrigerator. If the appliances are not installed or included, make sure your buyer measures the space to ensure that they will not have to purchase a custom (i.e., expensive) appliance.

Kathy did some quick research and found that the price of a custom-sized stove was around $1,000 (a decent typical-sized stove should cost around $500). We asked the seller to replace the stove, but he refused. The listing agent also refused to contribute toward solving the problem. So, I opened my checkbook and split the cost of the new stove with Kathy. Was it my fault? No. Was it my problem? Absolutely.

In Defense of the Open Checkbook Policy

In the above example of Kathy's Stove, how do you think Kathy would have felt about me, had I just shrugged my shoulders and let her absorb the cost of the new stove? Sure, she knew it wasn't my fault the stove didn't fit, but she still had every right to expect me to fix the problem for her. When the seller and listing agent refused to contribute to the cost of a replacement stove, I had two choices. I could continue to bully them by threatening to terminate the contract, or I could step up to the plate and help her buy the stove. (Or, of course, the third option, just shrug my shoulders and sheepishly walk away with my commission check.)

You might be saying to yourself "Well, that's because she (meaning me) is shy—she doesn't have the guts to fight it out," and I see your point. However, I don't consider a "lack of guts," used in this context, to be such a bad thing. I like to sleep at night, and if I can avoid an avoidable confrontation, I'll do it in the interest of expediency and peace of mind. Were the seller and listing agent wrong? In my opinion, yes, they were dead wrong. Was I willing to risk all the good will I'd built up with Kathy by starting an ugly battle that I would likely lose? Apparently not.

But having soul isn't synonymous with being a pushover, so lest you believe that the Open Checkbook Policy somehow implies that I think soulful salespeople don't stick up for themselves, let me set you straight. Sure, it's soulful to care enough about your client to be willing to spend your "own" money to solve their problem, but it's also often in your best interest too. When you're crazy-busy, you need to choose which battles to fight and which battles to take the easy way out. If you can buy your way out of a problem instead of spending lots of hours and lots of energy, sometimes it's the wiser choice. Your time is valuable too.

Another benefit of having your own Open Checkbook Policy is that it will help give you peace of mind in those times where you really need a closing. Many potential deal-breaking problems in a real estate transaction can be solved by throwing money at them. While it's not a habit you want to get into, it's good for you to know that if you have to, you can ensure yourself a closing by opening your checkbook.

You will run into these situations many times in your career. Each time, you will have a decision to make. Trust your gut—do what feels right to you. Legally, it's not your duty to take financial responsibility for others' mistakes, but every once in a while, it might just be the right thing to do.

Chapter Twelve

■ ■ ■ ■ ■

special types of sales

Selling New Construction

As a buyer agent, you may be involved in helping your buyer client purchase a home from a builder. In most cases, this is easy money for you. It's easy unless the builder is a flake, but even then, it's probably less stressful than a traditional real estate transaction. You don't have a large role in the process and the "seller" (the builder) isn't nearly as emotional as a regular home seller can be.

Here are some answers to questions you may have about selling new homes:

Will the builder honor my relationship with my buyers if they look at the home without me present (that is, will I get paid?)

Don't fret, this happens all the time. Most new home builders have a policy that buyers must register their agent with the builder on their first visit to the site. You don't usually have to be with your buyers, but they must declare in writing that they have a buyer agent when they sign in at the model home. If they don't, and they subsequently purchase a home from the builder, the builder does not have to pay you a commission, regardless of any buyer agency agreement you may have with your buyer.

When (not if) you get a call from the buyer you've driven all over town telling you about the great new home he found, just call the sales office right away.

Don't be afraid to make the call; on-site sales people have heard it a hundred times. They will almost always let you in on the deal. If they won't, well, you learned something. Real estate is a constant learning experience, in case you haven't noticed.

What is my role in the sales process?

You will be given a disclosure from the on-site salesperson explaining your duties as the buyer's representative. Usually you must attend the signing of the contract, the final walk-thru and the closing. The builder's representative handles everything else. You don't need to go to the design center with your buyer to pick out flooring, attend construction walk-thru's or meet with the buyer's lender.

Are the builder's prices negotiable?

In my experience, no. The market may change or vary by region, but unless you hear otherwise from your broker, don't feel that you need to earn your fee by negotiating the price. Builder contracts are rarely negotiable in any way. You'll just frustrate yourself and your buyer by asking for something the on-site sales person can't give you.

Should the buyer use the builder's lender?

Probably. If the home builder is a big company (not a small local builder), they may own a mortgage company and will offer incentives for your buyer to use their own lenders. These incentives can be substantial; I've seen incentives as high as $30,000. Your buyer can't turn that down and your own lenders can't compete, obviously. Even small builders usually have an independent preferred lender who will offer smaller incentives—perhaps a no-closing cost loan or a credit toward upgrades.

SHOULD I USE THE HOME BUILDER'S LENDER?
by Gary Miljour

Homebuilders are offering so many incentives today, just to get your signature on the contract. They may throw in a free pool, incentives as high as $20,000.00 to $30,000.00 and no closing costs. Heck, I heard one home builder advertising the other day on the radio, and they were giving away gifts worth about $100.00 just to come by and see their home models. Homebuilders are feeling the real estate crunch just like everyone else and they are playing the incentive game to sell homes, plain and simple.

Here is the catch. You must use the builder's "Preferred Service Vendors" to get these incentives. This means you will not have a choice on which lender you use. You must go with "their guy," no matter how expensive he or she is. So here is your choice: should I choose to take these incentives and pay more for lender services or, should I NOT take the incentives and pursue better lending alternatives?

Here is what I suggest you do:

First, before you ever step a foot into a new home subdivision, talk to a professional lender and get pre-qualified for a home loan. That way you know up front how much you can buy, what loan options are best for your situation and what the true costs of that mortgage are. Have your mortgage lender prepare a Pre-qualification Letter.

Before you contract on a new home, find out what incentives are being offered. Discuss these incentives with your real estate agent and make sure they are "REAL" incentives. Sometimes the incentives do not make much sense and just asking for a reduction in price might be better.

Find out if the builder requires the use of their "preferred lender." At this point, have your agent hand the builder your pre-qualification with your lender of choice and let them know you are already approved with another lender and would want to work with that person. The builder may just agree.

If the builder insists that you use their "preferred lender" in order to get the incentives, then you might try a couple of leveraging techniques.

Leveraging technique one:

Do not sign a contract unless they agree to let you use your lender of choice. Make them call their corporate office to check if they can make this happen. In today's market, builders really do want to make a sale, and if they think you will walk away from buying, they may give in.

Leveraging technique two:

Do not sign the contract until you are provided a Good Faith Estimate, Truth in Lending Disclosure and a Pre-qualification Letter from their preferred lender. If you see that the rates or programs are not competitive, you can call your builder and state that you do not want to use their lender because you do not like the loan they are offering you.

At this point, usually one of two things will happen. Either the builder will give in and let you use your own lender, or make their preferred lender match your lender's fee and rate structure.

Another reason to use the builder's lender is that some builders are real sticklers when it comes to the closing date. If the buyer is using an outside lender and the lender makes a mistake and can't close on the specified date, the builder just might threaten the buyer with default. If the buyer is using the builder's lender, and he misses the closing date, the builder can't really say anything. The builder's lender is also familiar with the project—the HOA, the financials, the appraisals.

One caveat, though. More than once I have seen a builder's lender do a bait-n-switch with my buyer (this has only happened with the big corporate builders). Right before closing, the lender announces that, for some obscure reason, he can't do the loan he promised, and therefore the buyer must put down more money or accept a higher interest rate.

I've never quite figured out why this happens so consistently—I don't think that the lenders do it on purpose. My best guess is that builder's lenders are somewhat sheltered from the real world of lending and aren't as experienced at recognizing and heading off potential problems early on.

As the buyer's representative, the best you can do is warn your buyer ahead of time that there may be loan issues at the last minute. If he has a relationship with another lender, it might be a good idea to recommend that he have a backup plan in place in case the builder's lender refuses to do the loan all together. If this happens, sometimes the builder will honor the incentive even if the buyer uses an outside lender.

Should my buyer hire a professional inspector?

YES YES YES! I always insist that my new home buyers have their home inspected by an independent inspector. Inspectors are trained to go through a home and identify issues and items that need correction; your buyer is not. Just because the builder has a signed Certificate of Occupancy from the city building inspector does not mean that the dishwasher is hooked up properly, that the windows open and shut smoothly, or that the sink stoppers are installed. It is not at all uncommon for the inspector to find dozens of action items and it is far easier (and more convenient) to have these items corrected before the buyer closes and takes possession.

Should I take buyer agency?

I do not believe in accepting buyer agency in new construction; I prefer to be a transaction broker (neutral party) when working with a builder. Why? Because in most cases, the buyer will have a direct relationship with the builder, one in which I have no control. They will meet with the builder without me, and I don't want to take responsibility for the builder's work. Additionally, I do not prepare the purchase contract and am not as intimately familiar with it as I would be with the standard contracts prepared by the state.

SELLING CONDOMINIUMS

Condominium sales present a few wrinkles in the process that you don't find in the sale of single family homes. Following are some questions you should get answered when involved in the sale of a condo, whether you're the listing agent or the buyer representative.

Is there a "working capital" requirement at closing?

I was burned once with this one. Many homeowner's associations require that buyers make a working capital deposit with the association at closing. This working capital requirement might be as much as three times the monthly HOA dues (e.g., if the monthly HOA fee is $175, the working capital due at closing would be $525). In Colorado, for instance, there is no mention of the working capital requirement in the standard contract so buyers are almost always caught by surprise the day before closing. If your buyer is counting pennies to come up with her down payment, this will be a nasty surprise. You, as the buyer's representative, might just get to pay the working capital deposit at the last minute to keep your closing together. If you are the listing agent of a condo, it's a good thing to know about; if the working capital deposit is more than a few hundred dollars, you might want to make the other agent aware of it up front to avoid last minute hassles.

How was I burned? I sold a $150,000 condo that had an $825 working capital deposit requirement that I wasn't aware of. The buyer's father felt that I, as the buyer's agent, should have told them about the requirement at the time they wrote the offer. I paid the $825.

Are there pet restrictions?

Some high-rise buildings do not allow pets or they impose limits on size.

Are there any move-in / move-out procedures?

Some high-rise buildings require notice for move-in/move-outs. They may not allow moves over the weekend and may require a damage deposit (sometimes non-refundable).

Confirm the HOA fees and what they cover!

Whether you represent the seller of a condominium or a buyer purchasing one, always call the association and confirm what the monthly/quarterly fees are and what exactly they cover. If you have a property listed for a long period of time, you need to periodically reconfirm the fees. If you are advertising the wrong amount, you could be liable for paying the difference, or even killing the sale if the buyer is at the top of his price range already. If your buyer gets to the closing table and finds out the fees have recently been raised, he may understandably get testy. And who do you think he is annoyed with...? It gets ugly and everyone looks bad—well, the real estate agents do anyway.

As you may suspect by now, I also created condominium checklists for my condominium buyers and sellers. They can be found in the Appendix and on my website. The first is the list of questions I use for myself when listing a condominium—I call the association and ask my questions, taking notes.

The second is a list of questions I use when I am representing a buyer; I usually call and ask the questions on behalf of my buyer, although I advise my buyer to do the same. In fact, I don't tell my buyers that I intend to make the call because I want to give them the responsibility for communicating with the HOA. Of course, if the HOA tells me something critical my buyers need to know, I will pass on that information, but in general, I give them the impression that verifying HOA information is up to them.

I learned this early in my career after I dutifully called an association president and was told that maybe, probably not, but perhaps there might be an assessment for new windows in the distant future. Right or wrong, I did not pass on this information to my buyer (probably wrong). Of course, within six months the association approved a $1,000 window replacement assessment and my buyer was furious with me. He felt that I had purposely withheld the information from him in order to secure my commission. That's hard to argue against and may have had some truth to it. Ouch. Like I said earlier, it happens.

FHA LOANS

For a few years, FHA loans fell out of favor due to the availability of a wide selection of other first-time buyer programs and 100% loans. However, as of this writing, many of those programs are gone, or not as easy to get, so I think we'll see a resurgence of the FHA loan.

FHA loans are great for first-time homebuyers who may not have the funds available for a significant downpayment and/or may have credit issues. To read more about the how's, why's, what's and who's of FHA, visit www.fhainfo. com. It's good reading, seriously!

Because FHA loans are government-insured, you'll find some nuances in the process that can catch you off-guard if you aren't prepared. Where you'll be most affected by FHA guidelines is during the appraisal process, which unfortunately means the issues come up later rather than sooner, since appraisals aren't usually done until late in the transaction.

While a conventional appraisal is simply a justification of value, an FHA appraisal goes much deeper. The appraiser must verify that the home is in good condition according to government standards. If the property does not meet these standards, the conditions must be corrected prior to closing.

Common red flags include peeling paint (a lead-based paint hazard), broken windows and missing hand railings. Any obvious structural condition (cracks in walls, sloping floors) will almost always kill your deal. The electrical system must be updated (no fuse boxes) and an older furnace must be certified. A rough-looking roof will be tagged, and all flat roofs must be inspected and certified by a roofer. Remember, all this is happening a week or so before closing! And, repairs must be made before closing—FHA rarely allows a repair escrow unless it's a weather-dependent item like a new roof.

Minor issues can usually be corrected in time. However, a seller might be understandably reluctant to make additional FHA-required repairs to a home after he has already negotiated the inspection. Many times, the buyer will spend his Saturday painting a home he doesn't own in order to get his loan approved. I once had to tell my seller that he had to replace the worn-out roof on a rickety lean-to porch to satisfy FHA. The worst part? The buyer was going to tear off the porch right after closing!

You need to be able to recognize potential problems long before the appraisal. If you are working with a fix-up buyer, try to dissuade him from using FHA financing. Warn your buyer that he may get to paint a house he doesn't own (in January) or pay for minor repairs (window replacement, hand railings) before closing. Sellers will usually do it, but be prepared for ones who won't.

The reason I say that a structural problem will almost always kill an FHA deal is because the appraiser will require a "Structural Certification" from a structural engineer. Now, in my experience, no structural engineer is going to "certify" a home that has some structural problem significant enough to be noticed by an appraiser. He will always require that some work be done by a licensed structural contractor and it won't be cheap or quick. It can be done—I once got some structural work completed in a week on a home that was almost in foreclosure, but I had a highly motivated seller.

When working with an FHA buyer, be sure that he or she selects a lender who has experience with FHA. These loans are enough different from conventional loans to warrant seeking out an expert.

■ ■ ■ ■ ■

so, you want to be a licensed assistant?

Easing into Your Real Estate Career

SPEAKING FRANKLY TO NEW LICENSEES...

You may have considered becoming a licensed assistant for an established agent, especially if you live in an area where real estate is not booming. Just for a while, you tell yourself, so you can learn the business without the risk. In a year or two, you'll go out on your own. I get a couple of calls a month from new licensees wondering if I'd be interested in hiring them as a buyer agent or licensed assistant.

Quite frankly, no, I'm not. Interested that is—but more on why that's so a little later.

Be warned, if you're brand new, I'm going to try to talk you out of going the licensed assistant route at this point in your career. It doesn't make sense for you or the agent you would work for.

A licensed assistant works under an active salesperson. Activities range from clerical inbox duties to working independently as a buyer agent. With the right combination of skills and personalities, a salesperson / licensed assistant team can be wildly successful. The wrong combination will be a waste of everyone's time, money, energy and emotion.

Who Makes a Good Licensed Assistant?

I, for example, have the skills (although not the personality) to be a great licensed assistant. A licensed assistant must be detail-oriented and enjoy paperwork. Not tolerate it, but actually enjoy it. She must be computer-literate. She must be reliable and organized. Not interested in the limelight—happy to play behind the scenes. Not interested in building her own business. In other words, a licensed assistant is everything a top salesperson typically is not. Well, duh—that's why the top salesperson needs her.

Therefore, why do you think you'd be a better licensed assistant than you would a full-time agent? Assuming you went to real estate school hoping to be a Top Dog someday, do you really think you have the personality to be the opposite: a behind-the-scenes-assistant? You're probably way more extroverted than I am and it would be hard for shy little me to give up control of my career and my income to be an assistant. It's just not in the makeup of a successful real estate agent.

If you're thinking, "Yeah, I can do it, for now," just beware that you may never break out of the assistant role. It can get pretty comfortable and a great licensed assistant can make good money. If you aren't willing or able to take the plunge into selling real estate now, what makes you think next year will be any different?

I guess what I'm trying to say is that, if you think you'll be a great licensed assistant, you'll probably never be a great (or happy) real estate agent. And vice versa. Sorry.

But It Gets Worse...

As a brand new licensee, you don't have much to offer a high producing salesperson. You don't know the systems, you may not know the market, you don't have any experience preparing contracts, CMA's, brochures or other marketing material. You've never held an open house. You've never set showings. You don't know how to order title work. You need to be trained in every single aspect of your job.

A Top Dog doesn't have the time or patience for that. And to actually pay you for the privilege of teaching you how to do your job? That goes against everything a top producing real estate agent believes in. Especially (and this is critical) if you've made it clear you intend to go out on your own someday. Why, oh why would a successful real estate agent take his time to train you, share his secrets and client list with you, even share his paycheck, knowing your goal is to be his competition someday?

Therefore, an ideal licensed assistant is an experienced agent who definitely no longer wants to sell. Perhaps she was never as successful as she dreamed she'd be, or she realized that she's not cut out for the stress of a full-time real estate agent's life. She's had her fun, now she's happy to play a support role.

IF YOU'RE BOUND AND DETERMINED...

So you still want to try this assistant gig? Okay, I'm happy to help. First, take a little time and get some training. If you're brand new and don't know how to work your local MLS, take a class or pay another agent to teach you. Make sure you know a desktop publishing program or two (e.g., Microsoft Publisher). Visit open houses and observe how the agents behave. Take a contracts class offered by the local board of Realtors®. Learn Top Producer or another contact management program. Know how to take and process digital photos. Read books about real estate. In other words, don't expect a successful real estate agent to train you in the basic functions of your job. Take the initiative to learn this stuff yourself.

I, for one, would be very impressed with you if you approached me with this can-do attitude, even if you were brand new.

Finding a broker to work for is likely a matter of networking. Successful real estate agents are too busy to make a concerted effort to find help. You will probably have to pretty much show up under her nose with a plan and a smile. Most overwhelmed agents I know all say they'd love to hire an assistant, but they just can't seem to get around to it. You might try making an appointment with the managing brokers of a few offices; they might know if there is someone in the office who would be interested in your services.

I'll tell you what will increase your street appeal to a potential broker/ employer—if you have a large circle of friends you'd be willing to share with him and let him add to his SOI—now that's worth something. However, if you intend to set off on your own in a few years, this is obviously a bad idea. If you're not willing to let your broker prospect to your SOI, just be sure to negotiate a referral fee if you bring in business yourself.

Real estate agents are notoriously cheap. So unless you really have something special to offer an agent, don't expect much in the way of compensation at first. As a new licensee, you have a lot to prove to a Top Dog or Top Dog Wannabe before they're going to be willing to make much of a financial commitment to you. If you're willing to work on commission only, you can probably negotiate a better deal for yourself. If you want a guaranteed salary, you will probably be offered an hourly rate just slightly higher than what the office receptionist makes. I hired an assistant once and paid her $12/hour, which was considered quite generous. And she had experience.

Again, if you're satisfied with $12/hour (just for now, of course), you may not be cut out for a career as a real estate agent. And that's okay!

Being a licensed assistant is an honorable career in itself, not a logical stepping stone between real estate school and a true real estate career. Because the skills, interests and personalities required to succeed are so different between the two jobs, it just doesn't make sense. If you want to sell real estate, go sell real estate. You can do it, I promise.

career development

Making Your Real Estate Career Work for You

PROSPECTING

Prospecting ...ahhh, prospecting. The bane of existence for some, the raison d`être for others. Some real estate agents proudly proclaim that they are sales(wo)men with a real estate license—in other words, they live to sell and real estate happens to be their product of choice. But it could be anything. Others, perhaps you among them, love to manage the process of a real estate transaction, but are a little bit less enthusiastic about the process of real estate prospecting.

To each his own. There's plenty of room in this business for all of us. But regardless of which "type" of real estate agent you are (salesperson or advisor), it's a fact that in order to succeed as a self-employed person, you need to have prospects, customers and clients.

I'm not going to waste your time describing prospecting methods I don't know anything about. You can find plenty of resources with information about cold-calling, door-knocking and leads-for-purchase programs. I'm certain that your broker, mentor or trainer has material for you to read on such strategies.

Following are the prospecting strategies I tried; some successfully, others not-so. Most of these methods fall under my overall SOI model, of course, since that's where the vast majority of my real estate business came from.

Web Marketing

In my opinion, the only good use of a website for a real estate agent is to provide an MLS search engine to buyers. No one on the web really cares about how wonderful you are, how awesome your company is or even about your fabulous listings. In order to drive people to your website, you need to offer something of value, and by far the most valuable thing your potential clients are looking for is information about homes for sale.

Web marketing is not cheap, so it probably shouldn't be a top priority for you until you're seeing a few dollars coming IN (rather than all going OUT). But if you are willing to respond quickly to leads and are aggressive (and organized) enough to follow up on them, you can do some serious business online.

If you're a reasonably good writer, you might want to consider starting a blog about your real estate market. A "blog" is simply an online journal, visible to the world, about whatever you want it to be about! It's not your regular website. Successful real estate bloggers write about their local market, as well as tidbits about their personal observations and experiences as related to selling real estate. The more personable and interesting you make your online persona, the more likely it is that you will attract like-minded clients to your door.

How do buyers and sellers find your blog? Well, that is a topic that is beyond the scope of this book, but for now, just know that if your blog is well-written, interesting and consistent (that is, you contribute to it regularly), you will eventually be rewarded with online inquiries.

Here is a blog ON blogging by one of Active Rain's (www.activerain.com) most popular bloggers.

Blogging Is Not High Tech
by Sarah Cooper

I recently switched brokerages. Everyone has been really nice, but I've realized I have a reputation as a "tech" person.

I am somewhat of a geek, but I'm no techie.

I've tried to explain a couple times that I'm not, but some of these people are still trying to get comfortable with turning a computer on and off. Maybe it's all relative and on a curve like that I get to claim some techiness.

Another thing I've tried to explain is that blogging is NOT a tech skill. It's WRITING.

Blogging is just talking through your keyboard. Blogging is not about HTML or WYSIWYG or any other jumble of letter that confuses the uninitiated. It's just about being able to express your thoughts. It's a creative outlet. It's about producing somewhat unique marketing that makes people WANT to come back and read more.

Yes, if you do it well, people will seek you out and come back on their own. Even when they don't need real estate!! See if your website can do THAT. (Yeah, I let my blog talk a little smack. BLOGS RULE.)

Anyone can blog. Anyone. You don't have to have special skills, but it will help if you have a basic grasp of the English language and use more than two fingers to type. Even those aren't required, you can muddle through and do just fine. You can blog about anything. Active Rain is great for increasing your online visibility and using it wisely can make you look like THE expert of your area. You can OWN your town if it's not spoken for, and if someone else is trying it you can sure give them a run for their money. Blogging and Active Rain can give you the edge.

Blogging is NOT about technical skill.

Blogging IS about being able to express your thoughts, being able to share what you see around you and letting people get to know you. Be true to yourself and speak from the heart and you will likely develop a following of people who have to see what happens next.

Don't be discouraged that locals don't comment. They rarely do. Every now and then I'll get an email from someone who reads my blog and appreciates what I have to say. Sometimes I'll get a request from someone out of town who misses something here and wants to see it again. No problem.

A nearby business is doing something fabulous? I reward them with some of my Google Juice. People remember the person that gives them great FREE advertising, don't doubt it.

My blog is whatever I want it to be. Hopefully when people read it they feel good about West Virginia and the people here. Hopefully my appreciation shines through.

Blogging is not about lines of code, it's all about getting the words from your heart or your head out in front of someone else's eyes.

Floor Time

Floor time is the opportunity to respond to inquiries that come into your office from advertising and For Sale signs. When you are on your floor time shift, you must be available to answer phone calls and talk with walk-in prospects and hopefully convert them into clients. To be effective on "floor" (as it's called), you'll need, at a minimum, to be familiar with the listings in your office. Of course, the more familiar you are with the market in general, the more productive your floor time will be. Some offices have tremendous floor activity; some have very little. If your office requires you to take floor time, well, then, I guess you'll do it! If it's voluntary, I recommend that you give it a fair shot to see if it works for you. Many floor calls are time-wasters, but certainly not all. If you take floor time a few times a month, you'll probably have three or four closings a year as a result. If your average commission is $5,000, that's not a bad use of your time!

Excerpted from
Your Successful Real Estate Career by Ken Edwards[5]

[If, while on floor duty,] an individual calls on a home-for-sale advertisement, he generally wants only one piece of information: the location of the property (assuming the price is stated in the ad). What he wants to do is what you

---

5   Kenneth Edwards, Your Successful Real Estate Career,
     AMACOM, 2007, page 90-91

would probably want to do under similar circumstances—drive by to see if it looks interesting.

No training program or text on real estate with which I am familiar advocates giving out the addresses in such instances. Some brokers absolutely refuse to let their agents do so. The fear is that the caller will drive by and, if he likes it, contact some other real estate company and buy through it.

There is an alternative approach that works well for some agents. Unless the homeowners have specifically requested that the address not be given out for drive-bys, give the callers the information they want. Proponents of this approach maintain that callers are so relieved that they don't have to agree to an appointment to get the information that they become easy to work with. In addition, there can be no argument that it certainly gets exposure for the seller's home, and that is your primary duty.

Farming

As you may know, "farming" refers to targeting a specific area and bombarding it with your marketing material. Some agents swear by it, others lost their shirts doing it. I did a little half-hearted farming, so I'm far from an expert, but I'll just say this...

1.   The best "farm" is a neighborhood where you already have or have had several listings. This gives you credibility. Otherwise, you're simply another pretty face on a postcard.

2.   If you're going to invest the money in geographic farming, you must commit to more than one mailing. As your name becomes more familiar within your farm, your chances of anyone caring about you will increase.

3.   Do open houses in the neighborhood, even if you have to do them for agents' other offices (if your broker allows that). Also, preview, preview, preview so that you are the neighborhood expert, not just the best neighborhood mailer!

GIVE THE PUBLIC A BREAK
by John MacArthur

I just got my mail. There were postcards from real estate agents telling me of home values in my area, telling me they were number one, telling me this is the ideal time to put my house on the market, telling me of the homes they have sold recently (although a quick check of the MLS indicates none of the homes has sold in the last 6 months), and advising me that they are the "neighborhood expert." I have been getting these cards for years. The names and faces change, but the mailbox overload continues.

This sort of marketing has a minimal return on investment. Do the real estate gurus really believe that if you inundate a market with these sorts of cards, you will land that listing? Of course, they will tell stories of agents who have had success. The majority of the agents that have invested money in these programs are not agents anymore. They went broke marketing. They took their toll on the tree population, kept printers in business and are now selling cars at CarMax.

New agents need to take a long look at how they treat "junk" mail in their personal lives. Most people will respond to coupons that offer buy one and get one free meals. Real estate agents don't offer to sell your home for half price if you get the neighbor to list at full price. Brokers across the nation extol the virtue of farming with postcards. Some firms will even offset your expense with credit for the postage. You still pay the bulk of the bill.

You show your family and friends the wonderful card. You sit back and know that 500 people saw your picture. You enjoy your 15 seconds of fame as your card is glanced at and dropped into the trash.

Of course, if the mail arrives just as a homeowner has decided to sell and the homeowner does not know an agent and the homeowner doesn't have any friends he can get a referral from and the homeowner has no co-workers he can get a referral from...he may call the number on the next card he receives. You just have to hope that yours is the one that hits at that moment under those conditions.

Last night, my wife and I were eating dinner when we were interrupted by the phone. It was an agent with a local firm who very politely told me that his company had a listing in the neighborhood and they had a great deal of interest at the open house and was wondering if I was thinking of selling or if I knew of any of my neighbors that might be interested in selling. Sounded good, but the agent works in my office and the home they were referring to was my listing and I sat in the open house they were referring to and there were no visitors. Bad luck for the agent.

The lie bothered me, but I knew he was reading from a script, so I let that go. I was more annoyed that he had chosen to "cold call" a neighborhood at the dinner hour. Of course calling at that time will catch more people at home, but common sense would indicate that interrupting a meal will not endear you to anyone.

There are lots of ways to market yourself effectively. You won't need to invade homes via the mail, phone or personal appearance. You won't have to spend yourself out of a career. You won't have to attend seminars and leave with an annual coaching contract. You won't have to buy every gimmick thrust on you at weekly sales meetings.

You can do it being yourself, working with your sphere of influence and focusing on being a real estate agent. You can be yourself and allow the public a long deserved break. You can do it now. You can do it if you are a new agent. You can do it if you have been an agent for years.

A strong dose of common sense will carry you further than all the cheerleading and direction of those that earn a sizeable chunk of the revenue you create. It is your decision how to practice your craft. I only ask...give the public a break.

For Sale by Owners (FSBO's)

As you may suspect, I never spent much effort prospecting to FSBO's. It's not that they are bad prospects; they can be wonderful clients, but I'm just too introverted to track down strangers and ask for business. Contrary to popular belief, FSBO's are not usually hostile to real estate agents in general, but they very well may be hostile to Old School agents who treat them as if they're stupid for trying to sell their home on their own. I would be hostile too! But if you're respectful and straightforward with them, you may very well get their business if they don't sell their home themselves. Or you may not. Many FSBO's have a friend in the business whom they have already promised their listing to after they try it on their own.

I'm not going to give you a step-by-step "program" for listing FSBO's; just use your own judgment. How would you like to be approached if you were trying to sell your home on your own? Respectfully? Honestly? Enthusiastically? So do that. Call up the FSBO, tell them you're a real estate agent and that you would love to meet with them to discuss the honor of marketing their home if they ever consider listing it with a real estate agent. Promise not to hassle them or take up too much of their time; try to leave any salesy tendencies out of the conversation. Just be real.

Expired Listings

I prospected for expired listings for a period of around six months. I wrote a nice letter, followed up by a postcard campaign of four postcards, mailed every three days, followed by another letter. I added the seller to my SOI and included them in any general mailings I did. I got exactly one listing as a result of my efforts and that listing expired again with me because the sellers weren't motivated. So, do I recommend prospecting to expired listings? Maybe, maybe not. Maybe you'll have more luck; I have heard many success stories from more charismatic agents who made more of an effort to actually speak to or even meet the sellers instead of depending on a mailing campaign. It's not my style to bother people, so I never attempted to personalize my approach beyond my postcards.

Newspaper Advertising and Real Estate Magazines

These get a big NO from me. But if your office pays for them, go ahead and take advantage. Just don't use your own valuable marketing dollars on general print advertising. It doesn't work and as fewer and fewer agents advertise this way, the rates just get higher. There are far more productive ways to spend your money—lunch dates, housewarming parties, even web marketing.

Housewarming Parties

If you're a social type, throwing a housewarming party for a good client is a fabulous way to prospect. For me, no way, I'm way too introverted to be a hostess at that sort of party, but most agents are much more party-animalistic than I am. My business partner once threw a housewarming party for a client and she was still getting business from it, three years later.

It's important to choose the right client for your party—someone who has a lot of friends, even better if you have a lot in common with your client so that it's likely you'd hit it off with her friends as well. And, ideally, the house you sold her is in a part of town that you're familiar with, so you can speak intelligently about the market in that area.

You want to be the hostess for the party, not just pay for it. You do the inviting (E-vites are great and you get more e-mail addresses for your SOI!), you show up early to help set up, you arrange for cleanup at the end of the party. And yes, you pay for the food and any decorations. Don't go overboard, but do make it a memorable party for the guests. This is not an opportunity for you to overtly market yourself, but believe me, you'll have plenty of chances to hand out business cards.

Dinner Parties

Dinner parties (or afternoon BBQ's) are great ways to take several friends "to lunch" all at one time. And, even for shy folks like me, an intimate gathering of friends is something to look forward to, not to be stressed over. Why not have four or five of the events over the next year? If you invite 8 different friends or couples to each, that's 32 to 40 people you subtly prospected to and had a good time doing it.

Let's think of some occasions to celebrate...how about your birthday? Your spouse's birthday? The Super Bowl? New Year's Eve? Your own housewarming party (even if you moved over a year ago!)? Even Valentine's Day? Go through your SOI and make a list of friends who would probably show up. Put a date or two on your calendar and start planning. Trust me, the money you spend on your dinner parties will be well worth it. I promise you, these parties will pay for themselves, many times over.

Three "Outings" a Week

Get out of the house or office! At least three times a week. Visit a new home community and chat with the on-site salespeople. Drop in on your buddy who bartends downtown, at a quiet time, so you can talk with him and say hello to the other workers there. Take your dog to the dog park. Attend Wednesday night Bible study. Volunteer at your local Humane Society or homeless shelter. Stop by your favorite mortgage broker's office to say hi. Go see your spouse or significant other at work and take a minute to say hello to everyone you see there. Hell, go get a massage, a facial, a brow-wax or a pedicure with a smile on your face.

Or—the absolute best business generating technique—are you ready? Plan a vacation. I guarantee that the week before you leave will be the busiest week of your life. Ask any experienced agent. It's foolproof.

I'll leave you with one more bonus strategy—when you're busy, go look for more. I know you'll be feeling overwhelmed, but that's the best time to prospect. You'll be glowing, with enthusiasm oozing out of every pore. Your attitude will be irresistible and the universe will respond with even more business for you. Nothing generates additional business like being too busy to handle more business.

Just don't whine about how busy you are, either to yourself or to anyone else. It's irritating and self defeating. Practice saying, "Business is unbelievable—I never thought I'd enjoy real estate so much!"

FINDING YOUR NICHE

Having a niche or a specialty will make your life as a real estate agent much more fun. It's so easy to market yourself when you truly have something special to say about your service, especially if you're shy about self-promotion.

By "niche" I don't really mean a geographic farm area, although you can certainly try that if you like. I don't like the idea of a farm because you should be getting most of your business from your SOI, who probably don't all live in the same neighborhood. If you have the marketing funds to bombard a certain geographic area with your advertising, go for it. But in my opinion, it's too expensive and too uncertain.

No, by "niche" I mean a market specialty you know a lot about that the majority of other agents haven't capitalized on. Your niche can be a certain category of buyers...or sellers...or properties. Or perhaps you'd like to learn more about a certain type of transaction, preferably one that is a little more difficult than "standard" transactions.

I am always looking for agents who specialize in buying foreclosures, selling pre-foreclosures and negotiating short sales because I have chosen not to work with these types of situations. Imagine...not only will you get the business of buyers and sellers interested in these services, but you'll also get referrals from other real estate agents! Other niche ideas—multi-family income properties, condo and townhouse conversions, older homes (older than 75 years), infill development, "difficult" properties (e.g., homes on busy streets), horse properties, pool properties, golf course homes, downtown lofts, rent-to-own buyers, VA buyers, to name a few.

For a while my niche was listing vacant homes. I fell into my niche because of all the fix-n-flip investors I worked with in the late 1990's and because I also owned a home staging company that furnished and decorated vacant homes. Is marketing vacant homes brain surgery? Nope. But there are special considerations to be handled such as lawn care, snow removal, light bulb replacement, temperature control and vandalism. Also, vacant homes typically appear smaller than furnished homes and definitely don't photograph as well. I've always preferred marketing vacant homes because I don't have to deal with sellers who are uncooperative with the marketing and showing process. It is a great specialty for an introverted real estate agent.

I didn't decide one day to be a specialist in vacant properties; it just sort of happened. To find your niche...open your mind. You don't have to pick one today or even tomorrow, just keep it in the back of your mind. Maybe you find yourself working with a military family who refers you to another military family who refers you again. Voila! Suddenly you can market yourself as the local military base expert and it's not hype! You truly will understand the special needs of a military family, along with the nuances of VA financing. This knowledge is more valuable to the marketplace than you might think. Believe it or not, even seasoned real estate agents don't know it all. I know nothing about VA loans, foreclosures, commercial real estate or land sales, and I'm thrilled to refer perfectly good buyers and sellers to agents who specialize in these areas.

101 Niche Marketing Ideas
(well, maybe not 101, but a lot)
by Janie Coffey, Papillon Real Estate, LLC

- Pet friendly (for dogs, horses, other animals)
- Lake or river property
- Boating (room for boat storage, bay access, ocean access, etc.)
- Golf
- Historic homes
- Homes with additional income property on them
- Live/work/play (i.e., retail or office with a living component)
- Vacant homes
- Fixer-uppers/handy-man specials
- Low maintenance homes
- Garden homes
- Homes on air-parks (for private air planes)
- Vacation homes
- 55+ Communities
- Small and efficient
- Green and/or energy efficient homes
- Specific architectural style
  (brownstone, adobe, farm house, Victorian, art deco, etc.)
- Designed by a specific architect
- Homes with pools
- Homes with aqua-culture, i.e., specialty fish ponds
- Homes with tennis or basketball courts
- Homes located where you can walk to entertainment and stores
- Artsy/bohemian areas and homes
- Homes that can accommodate RV or other large vehicle parking
- Homes with large workshops for hobby crafters, auto hobbyists, etc.

- Homes close to outdoor activities such as hiking, biking, etc.
- Homes prepared for certain local natural disasters
  (e.g., hurricane, tornado, flood resistant prone)
- Lofts
- Bed-n-breakfasts
- Ghost houses
- Housing for student rentals
- Ski and other winter sport homes
- Returning to the downtown urban core
- Coastal cottage and beachfront homes
- Homes good for birding
- One of a kind homes
- Mountainside homes
- Farms, groves, etc.
- Gated communities
- Auctions, foreclosures, short sales, condos, estate homes
- ADA (American's with Disabilities Act) Accessible
- Island Property
- Properties for celebrities such as movie stars and athletes
  (often need heightened security features and privacy)
- Properties for musicians
  (often need special rooms, sound proofing, etc.)
- Homes with interesting original purposes
  (e.g., firehouses, factories, churches, etc.)
- Historic homes that need to be moved
  (you can also offer the moving service)
- Homes that have in-law homes or quarters on them
- Homes that have large wall space to accommodate art collections
- Homes that have extra large garages for other
  features for the auto enthusiasts

GOAL-SETTING

I'll admit I'm not a big goal-setter. I just work hard most of the time and good things seem to come of it. However, I do notice that if I will be publicly rewarded for reaching a goal, I might just direct my efforts toward meeting that goal and I usually succeed. If you're the same way, look for opportunities within your office to get some "atta-boys," such as annual awards for production or number of listings and/or sales, monthly in-office "agent of the month" awards, or newspaper announcements for the top producing agent of the month or quarter. Perhaps you can make a deal with your broker that you will hit certain goals by certain deadlines and ask him or her to monitor your progress and keep you accountable.

The first company I worked for had an award at the end of the year for every agent who had at least one listing and one buyer sale each and every month. It didn't count if you had five listings and no buyer sales; no, you had to have one of each. I wanted that plaque to hang on my wall, and I got it. Some months I was beating the bushes to find a listing, but I managed to make it happen and this was only my first full year in the business. Another year, further on in my career, I realized on October 1 that I was $50,000 away from making the Re/Max Platinum Club and, by golly, I wanted that designation. So, shy-little-me got on the phone and somehow drummed up $50,000 worth of business, all of which had to close by December 31. And it did. Yay for me!

Anyway, give this goal-setting business a try, but make the goals meaningful to you. I don't advise making specific production goals—as in "I'll sell five houses this month" or "I'll have three closings every month." The problem with these types of goals is that much of what it takes to meet those goals is out of your control, or should be.

What do I mean by that? I mean that if you are working with buyers, the inventory of the market is out of your control. The perfect home for your buyer may not be available right now or your buyer may need more time to decide. It is not soulful to push your buyer to contract on a home, just so you can meet your goal.

Likewise, there's not much you can do above and beyond your regular marketing to get your listings sold and closed within your specific parameters. You don't want to motivate yourself to manipulate your clients for your own purposes; you might find yourself forgetting who you represent. However, you can motivate yourself to go get buyers and listings; you just can't necessarily control when they buy, sell or close.

So instead of making general production goals, make your goals a little more specific and 100% within your control. For example, how do you feel about these annual goals?

By the end of March:

- Adding 40 people to your SOI
- 100 homes previewed
- 3 new home neighborhoods visited
- 15 lunch dates
- 25 "outings"
- 5 open houses
- 3 SOI e-mails sent out
- 1 mailing that included your business card
- 1 continuing education class
- 50 thank you cards sent

By the end of June:

- 80 names added to your SOI
- 200 homes previewed
- 6 new home neighborhoods visited
- 30 lunch dates
- 50 "outings"
- 10 open houses
- 6 SOI e-mails sent out
- 2 mailings that included your business card
- 3 continuing education classes
- 100 thank you cards sent
- 1 dinner party for friends

By the end of December:

- 140 names added to your SOI
- 400 homes previewed
- 10 new home neighborhoods visited
- 60 lunch dates
- 100 "outings"
- 20 open houses
- 10 SOI e-mails sent out
- Your two mailings plus an end-of-year mailing (calendar, newsletter, holiday card, etc.)
- 6 continuing education classes
- 200 thank you cards sent
- 2 dinner parties for friends
- 1 housewarming party for a client

These goals are all completely doable and 100% within your control. If you meet these goals, you will have consistent business, no question. Did you notice that I didn't include any cold-calling or any for-sale-by-owner prospecting? If you want to add some more traditional prospecting methods into your goals, go for it. But if you don't want to, don't worry about it—you'll have plenty of good business without bothering strangers.

If you have business coming in regularly, go ahead and include some production goals. But again, don't make goals that will encourage you to pressure your clients inappropriately. Perhaps you can set a goal of $70,000 gross commission for the year and simply monitor your progress toward that goal every month. Or, strive to increase your commission split by a level or two (if your split is determined by your production). If you're not on track, take a look at your prospecting goals (above) and make sure you're meeting those.

A few more (important) things to be doing right now...

START BUILDING YOUR TEAM

When I talk about Your Team, I am not referring to your assistant or your buyer agent. I'm talking about outside contractors in your life who love you (because you give them business and make sure they get paid promptly) and will make your life as a real estate agent infinitely easier—they'll save your ass and your commission check and make you look goooood. You'll provide exceptional service, dramatically increase your closing ratio (i.e., reduce the number of sales that crash) and sleep much better at night. Once you have your team in place, you'll wonder how anyone practices real estate without one.

Here are the players:

Handyman

Every real estate agent must have a good handyman on call. Every real estate agent must have a good handyman on call. Every real estate agent must have a good handyman on call. He will save your commission over and over again. Find him, treat him well, pay him immediately. Be his top priority when you call on him. How agents operate without a great handyman is beyond me. A good handyman can handle plumbing and electrical repairs, carpentry, painting (although many choose not to paint) and garage door remote programming.

Bob is my handyman. He's personable, presentable and reasonable. He'll drive across town to fix an overflowing toilet and charge $20. He can fix anything and my clients adore him. I once had a plumbing issue with a 100-year-old clawfoot tub that three plumbers told me couldn't be fixed. Bob stewed over the problem for an hour or so and came up with a solution for about $70. If you can find a Bob in your town, he is like gold to you and your business. Don't let him get away.

House Cleaner

You can survive without a house cleaner, but I don't recommend it. You need someone reliable who is available on relatively short notice. Again, find her, treat her well, pay her immediately. More than once I found myself cleaning a home on the day of closing because the seller didn't do it. Or was sent a cleaning bill because my listing was "filthy" at the time of possession and the buyer had to hire Maids-R-Us, at $60/hour.

HVAC Contractor

You must have a good, reliable, reasonably priced heating and air conditioning contractor on your team. In Colorado, heating system concerns are among the biggest reasons real estate transactions fall apart at inspection. Ideally, find a one-man operation that needs your business, rather than a big company that does radio advertising. My independent HVAC contractor has replaced 100-year-old cast iron octopus style furnaces for as little as $2,500, when others charge as much as $9,000. Heating contractors can usually help you out with plumbing issues too, leading me to my next category...

Plumber and Electrician

Depending on the expectations in your market, you may not use the services of a licensed plumber or electrician as often as you think you might. A good handyman can handle most of the plumbing and electrical work you'll run into. The nice thing about having a handyman do your work for you (besides his lower rates!) is that he can clean up any mess that he makes while doing the repair—for example, if he has to open up a wall to fix a leaking pipe, he can put the wall back together and paint it. Most licensed specialty contractors don't do that—they leave it for the homeowner to deal with.

The only times I ever hire a plumber or electrician is if a buyer or seller insists on having a licensed contractor make a repair at inspection or if a repair item requires a city permit that can only be pulled by a licensed plumber or electrician.

Roofer

Roof replacement prices vary widely and in most towns there will be a few roofers who cater to the real estate community. They are ready, willing and able to inspect a roof (hopefully at no cost) on a moment's notice and provide an estimate of repair or replacement in a timely manner. They know that more business will be forthcoming if they do a good job for you, so ask around your office to see if there are, indeed, a few "real estate agent roofers" in town.

Structural Engineer and Structural Contractor

If you live in a town where you will run into structural issues with the homes you sell, you'll need to have the names of both a structural engineer and a structural contractor. There's a difference between the two. A structural engineer evaluates a home and provides technical recommendations to correct structural deficiencies. The engineer does not make repairs and therefore generally has no idea of the cost of his or her recommendations. A structural contractor, on the other hand, is the person who actually makes structural repairs and can provide recommendations, as well as cost estimates.

Personally, I dislike the structural engineering racket. Many engineers are dour old codgers who hate older homes and love to kill perfectly good real estate deals. These guys scare buyers to death with predictions of gloom and doom if they don't make the recommended repairs right away and, since the buyers don't know how much repairs cost, they assume the worst. Whenever possible, I try to get my structural contractor in first. He tends to be surprisingly calming and his repair estimates are almost always far lower than the guesstimate provided by the structural engineer.

Other contractors to have on file are: a staging professional, a house painter and a hardwood floor installer/refinisher.

Here are a few more members for your team:

Mortgage Brokers

You'll need two or three good mortgage brokers. If you've worked with a mortgage broker in the past on personal home purchases (and were satisfied), by all means call him (or her). Ask your friends, your associates.

What makes a mortgage broker "good"? Responsiveness! And

Where Do I Find My Team?

You aren't going to find them in the phone book. The team members you are looking for can't afford a big splashy yellow page ad. The best way to find reliable contractor-types is by keeping your antennae up. Look at bulletin boards in grocery stores, classified ads in the newspapers under "services" and, if you have any builder friends, ask them whom they use. If you are on the buyer side of a real estate transaction, notice whom the listing agent used for any negotiated repairs. Once you have found one good contractor, ask him—he'll likely have friends in the other trades who would love to have your business. It's trial and error, but you will find them. And you will wonder how you ever closed a sale without them.

creativity, the willingness to work with less-than-cherry borrowers, someone who is a good fit for your personality. None of which you'll know up front; you'll just have to test drive them. The good news is that there are mortgage brokers on every corner, and they'll be thrilled to get your business.

Other Real Estate Agents

Yes, other real estate agents can be valuable members of your team. Think referral fees. Free money! I choose not to work with foreclosures, short sales, commercial property, vacant land or rent-to-own buyers. But believe me, I have great resources in the real estate community for these types of transactions.

Twenty to twenty-five percent commission for making a phone call? Sounds good to me.

Don't spend a lot of time searching for real estate agents to refer to—they will cross your path during the course of doing business. Make friends with them and keep their contact information current.

Home Inspectors

Oh, to have three great inspectors on my referral list! Right now I have one. If he's not available, my backups will do, but I'm just not as confident. I have gone through dozens of inspectors and found most of them less than satisfactory. Either they're classic deal-breakers (every house is a money pit) or, at the opposite extreme, they're in and out in under an hour. Finding good home inspectors is an ongoing challenge. Get referrals from other agents and your broker.

CONTINUING EDUCATION

Your first year is a good time to start acquiring designations. You have the time to spend in class (at least more than you'll have in years two to five), you'll hopefully learn something and at the end you'll have a fancy symbol to add to your business card. However, something to consider is that you may not "need" continuing education credits in your first year, so the money you spend on such courses will not benefit you in that regard.

The GRI (Graduate Realtor® Institute) and the ABR® (Accredited Buyer Representative) are two good programs for residential agents. The classes are not too expensive and most metropolitan areas offer the programs year round. If you live in a smaller town, you might have to travel for the classes or take them online. If at all possible, take the classes in person. Online learning is fine for last-minute continuing education (CE) credit acquisition (oops, the deadline is next week?), but not so great for actually learning the material.

By taking the courses live and in person, I promise you will learn more and come away with some great ideas. It's also interesting to hear the chatter of other real estate agents, although at times you'll want to pull your hair out at some of the stupid, irrelevant questions and un-soulful commentary.

Many real estate boards offer ongoing continuing education classes on a variety of interesting topics. Classes on HUD homes and foreclosures could open new avenues of business for you or, conversely, convince you (as they did for me) that you don't want to mess with them. Take a class on 1031 Exchanges. You don't need to be an expert, but you need to know what they are.

Ethics and agency classes are always fun—if you like hearing how all your Standard Operating Procedures are illegal and/or unethical. You can always recognize a student fresh from an agency class—they have a dazed look on their face caused by the realization that they're just an audit or complaint away from professional disgrace. A Legal Issues class will do this for you too.

Aside from the GRI and ABR® classes, many other opportunities to learn stuff about real estate will come your way. Take advantage of them as often as you can. Many title companies offer free educational seminars to real estate agents, in the hopes of earning their business. Often these classes are even eligible for CE credit. Your Board of Realtors® probably offers periodic classes taught by local real estate agents—these can be hit or miss, but some of my best ideas have been born in these classes (see below). Local real estate license schools probably offer elective courses, as do community colleges. Y'know all that junk you get in your office mail box? Go through it periodically to see if you got any flyers or brochures offering classes that interest you.

Now, that's another topic. Interest. Should you take classes that sound as if they'll bore you out of your mind but are probably "good for you"? Yeah, probably. Well, maybe. It depends on the class. For example, I took a foreclosure class once and halfway through, literally walked out because I realized I couldn't have cared less about foreclosures. Believe it or not, that was a good lesson for me to learn; now whenever a potential buyer asks me about foreclosures, I just say, "I don't do foreclosures, but let me refer you to someone who does." It was worth "wasting" half a day to discover that. Of course, some instructors are so awful they can make a potentially interesting subject deadly.

I'll share a little secret with you though...even in the most worthless classes, I always come away with some incredible ideas. No, not from the teacher or even the other students, but as a direct result of my boredom and restlessness. I hate to sit in a chair for eight hours. I'm a baaaad "student." So I always take a notepad and a calculator. While the teacher is droning on, my mind goes to work. Ideas flood my brain.

Perhaps it has something to do with being physically trapped; my mind insists on being free and just has a field day. I write my ideas down in my notepad, expand upon the good ones, discard the stupid ones; some days I've walked away with 20 or more pages filled up with my scribbles. The calculator will come in handy in case you're inspired to prepare a budget for yourself, calculate how much money you have in your pipeline (if all your prospects go to closing, how much money will you make?) or set financial goals for yourself.

At a time when I had about a dozen listings, I spent one boring CE class calculating how much money I would make if I "double-ended" all my current listings. I think it was some crazy number in the $100,000's. So, I spent that time in class brainstorming (with myself) all the ways I could increase the odds of selling my listings myself. Now, as you may recall from Chapter Nine, double-ending listings is not as fun as it sounds and I never put my action plan into play. But it was a great way to productively get through a boring class. Keep your notes—when you look back on them at a later date, you'll be surprised at the brilliance therein!

And of course, if you're brand new, go get some training on your MLS and contract software right away. Even if you have to hire another soulful agent in your office to train you, you must be proficient on these systems before you can honestly call yourself a real estate agent.

Another class you might want to investigate is formal training on your contact management software. If you use Top Producer, for example, check with your sales representative to see if he or she has any classes scheduled. I promise you that there are features you never knew existed and could possibly change your business.

COMMIT TO A CONTACT MANAGEMENT SYSTEM (CMS)

Speaking of your contact management system, you might remember that earlier, we briefly discussed the fact that you will need to commit to some sort of computerized system to manage your contact database.

There are several different CMS's to choose from; some are real estate-specific, such as Top Producer, Agent Office and Realty Juggler. Many other not-real-estate-specific systems are also available.

The product you choose will depend on your budget, your level of techno savvy-ness and your preference for delivery format. Some products, like Top Producer, are hosted on a server and can be accessed on any computer. Others, like Agent Office, are installed on your desktop. Top Producer requires an annual contract and (currently) costs around $35/month. Agent Office (currently) requires a fee of around $300 with no monthly charges, although you will need to pay for periodic updates.

If your budget doesn't allow for the purchase of a CMS at this time, you can use Outlook or Excel for free. Many agents use these programs and are satisfied with them. As your business grows, however, you may want to consider upgrading to a more robust, real-estate-specific product.

I used Top Producer and was happy with it, although it's not the most user-friendly product on the market. At the time of this writing, I am in the process of investigating other CMS products that are easier to learn and use. I may decide the Top Producer really is the best, or I may find another equally powerful program that I can heartily recommend. Stay tuned.

I recommend using a CMS for two main purposes. First, to enter and maintain your SOI, of course. However, as your career picks up speed, the more important use you may have for your CMS is to keep track of your listings and pending sales.

All my active listings, buyers under contract and listings under contract were entered into my CMS with a comprehensive follow-up program I created from my checklists that are described throughout this book. Every day I checked my To-Do list online and nothing ever slipped through the cracks.

When you only have a few deals going on, this may seem more complicated than it's worth. But when (not if) your business takes off, you won't have time to figure out the program, so practice now! At one point in my career, my partner and I had 40 listings and 20 pending sales and I never broke a sweat keeping track of dates, deadlines and duties.

I still use my CMS to track personal dates, such as reminders regarding my rental properties (shut down the sprinkler system in October, change the furnace filters every month, etc.), reminders to give my dogs their heartworm pills, even reminders to pay my bills when I get really busy.

The best website I've found to learn more about and compare the different CMS programs is www.GaryDavidHall.com.

■ ■ ■ ■ ■

some final thoughts,
a few more stories & last minute advice

DON'T GET TOO CAUGHT UP IN ONE PROSPECT

E specially when you're new, you tend to see everyone you meet as prey. If they have a real estate need, you're determined to be the one to meet it and you'll take it personally if they don't use you. Try to keep things in perspective and don't get too upset if someone you know uses another agent, or otherwise "cuts you out of the deal." If you behave badly, you will be embarrassed years down the road at your lack of sensitivity to your prospect's situation and needs. I hope you are, anyway.

Brian was one of my biggest investor clients and my main source of referrals in my early years. In my second year of business, Brian bought a townhouse (using me as his buyer agent) as a fix-n-flip investment. Of course, I was counting on listing the townhouse when the renovation was completed, and since I was relatively new to real estate, this was a Big Deal to me.

Well, one thing you'll have to get used to if you work with investors is that they are hoping for a profit (duh)—the bigger the better. If they can eliminate real estate fees, which are a huge cost of doing business for an investor, they'll quickly cut you out of the deal. During renovation, their project may attract a lot of unwanted (in your opinion) attention from buyers and real estate agents. Unfortunately, you can't stand guard on "your" listing 24 hours a day to protect it from intruders. Your investor might get cocky (you would too, admit it) and figure he doesn't need you.

Brian did end up selling the renovated townhouse himself, to a buyer who walked in off the street. He didn't have to pay anyone a commission, saving himself around $9,000. I was heartbroken and for a moment considered terminating our professional relationship.

Is this tacky or what? Luckily, I handled it professionally (sheer willpower on my part) and our relationship continued. Always, when a client does something that takes money out of your pocket, try to see the situation through his eyes before you react. What he did was probably reasonable, and besides, it's done now...move on.

Here's another story. During my first year in real estate, a work associate from my past life listed her home for sale...with another agent who happened to be the dominant agent in the neighborhood. I was, again, heartbroken. Her explanation to me was that she didn't want to hire a "friend" (a tactic you'll encounter throughout your career; many times it will work for you when a "stranger" prospect hires you instead of their best friend).

In retrospect, I'm sure she didn't want to hire a brand new agent, and I can't blame her. But I got mad and wasted lots of emotional energy being mad. Get used to it. Be grateful for all the friends who do hire you, even though they know perfectly well you probably aren't the most qualified. Soon enough you will be able to convince your friends to hire you not just because they like you, but because you're an extraordinary real estate agent.

When you get blown off or cut out, go ahead and be heartbroken for an hour or two. If you really want to, you can lose a night's sleep over it. Sure, you might have wasted some time, you may be counting on the commission to pay your mortgage (you know better though, don't you?), but these things happen. It's a tradeoff...sometimes deals fall into your lap with little effort on your part. Don't destroy a friendship and/or your credibility by pouting or fussing. It gives real estate agents a bad name, and certainly reduces your chance of getting referrals from this person. Graciously accept defeat, and offer to help if you can. After all, you would probably have done the same thing in a similar situation. Remember that.

PLAY FAIR WITH REFERRALS

In a desperate quest for a paycheck, real estate agents sometimes do things that are embarrassingly self-serving. We all did them and you will too. Things that later in your career make you cringe (I hope).

When I was new in the business, I found myself frantically pursuing referral fees. Just because I was now "in Real Estate," I felt entitled to collect money from the agents who already had relationships with friends and family members. My older sister was a real estate investor in California who regularly purchased high-dollar properties. I actually approached her to see if she thought her agent would mind paying me referral fees on my sister's deals. Is that tacky or what? But not that unusual.

Throughout your career you will pay referral fees to other agents who did nothing to earn them, most commonly a relative in another state who happens to have a real estate license. Even if you found your client all on your own, even if she's your best friend, you'll be asked to pay a referral fee. It's your call. As a new agent, you will probably just shrug your shoulders and be grateful to have any business at all. Later you might be willing to take a stand or let the prospect go. Just hope that all the referring party wants is a piece of the financial action and not to "help out."

Some of the most miserable deals I've ever had were representing buyers whose mothers were real estate agents. Nothing you do is good enough, you can't negotiate hard enough, your contracts will never be written strong enough. She will second-guess every move you make and fill her precious darling's head with all kinds of nonsense that you'll somehow have to tactfully deprogram. It's a nightmare.

Anyway, back to referrals. Don't ask for referral fees you didn't earn. It's beneath you. Also, if you're going to refer your client to another agent, please do a little homework and make sure it's a reasonable match. Make a phone call or two. Don't just open your handy-dandy Re/Max Referral Catalog and give out a phone number—a little pre-screening will go a long way toward ensuring a satisfied client and thus an eventual referral check in your pocket.

With regard to referrals, I ask for (and pay out) 20% for listings and 25% for buyers. I feel that since listings typically cost the listing agent money out of pocket, it's fair to pay (and take) a little less.

You Can't Be All Things to All People

On a drive across Kansas one sunny afternoon, I was listening to a motivational real estate tape in my car. The format consisted of agents calling in with anecdotes, questions and helpful tidbits. This day the topic was handling referrals.

One of the callers asked the question: "What do I do if I get referrals for buyers looking for homes that are outside of my area of expertise?"

I was stunned by the moderator's answer, which was (in effect)...

"You must qualify the buyer before you waste your (emphasis mine) time driving all over the countryside with him. If you're going to drive an hour or more away from home, that buyer better be a real buyer, not just someone kicking tires."

TIRADE ALERT!

Now hold on just a minute. Waste your time? How about the buyer's valuable time? What business does this agent have taking on a buyer outside of her "area of expertise"? When I hire a real estate agent, it's because she is the local expert. She knows the nuances of the neighborhoods, the local market trends. She can tell me if a home is a good deal or if it's overpriced, or if there is a gas station being built on the corner. No matter how good you are, if you don't know the market, you have no business selling homes there. In fact, even as an experienced real estate agent, I always hire a local real estate agent when I buy property outside of Denver.

If you agree to take on a buyer who is looking for homes outside your area, will you be willing to race out every time a new listing comes up, and, as a corollary, will you be tempted to push your buyers to purchase something on your first or second trip just so you don't have to make the drive again? That isn't fair to your buyers. In my humble opinion, agents do a serious disservice to their clients by agreeing to work in an area that they are unfamiliar with.

I recently purchased a few homes in L.A. (Lower Alabama) and talked with four real estate agents prior to selecting one to work with. The first agent I spoke with was referred to me by a friend, and admitted she was not an expert in the area I was considering. I was uneasy about this because I didn't know anything about the area either and wanted an expert to show me around. When she made the comment, "Well, we can learn about Dothan together," I knew I needed to find help elsewhere. Please be fair to your prospects. If you're not the expert, refer them to someone who is. A 25% referral fee for making a phone call sounds like a pretty good deal to me!

THE STORIES OF THREE GREAT REAL ESTATE AGENTS

I've had the privilege of being represented by three great agents in my personal real estate transactions. I'd like to give them public kudos here, and describe what, in my opinion, made them outstanding.

Joan Hart in Steamboat Springs, Colorado; Millie Miller in Dothan, Alabama and Nicole Lincoln in Houston, Texas.

It's an eye-opening experience for real estate professionals to hire other real estate professionals to represent them in a sale or purchase of property. Even if you don't want investment property in other locations, it's almost worth going through the process just to remind yourself what it's like to be so dependent on your real estate agent. You'll come away from the experience with a renewed commitment to look after the needs and protect the vulnerabilities of your own clients.

As I describe why I'm so crazy about these three agents, the word that comes to mind is, again, respect. All three of them respected me as a client, aside even from being a fellow real estate broker. They honored my wishes, considered my opinions, respectfully answered my "silly" questions. At no time did they ever question my judgment or make me feel like a nuisance. And believe me, I can be as annoying and demanding as any other out-of-town buyer! They all made me feel that I was their most important client; I had their complete attention when I needed it.

A Great Listing Agent...

Joan sold an investment townhouse that I purchased pre-construction and eventually flipped for a $30,000 profit. It was a complicated sale. We marketed and sold the townhouse prior to completion, so not only did she get to handle the listing side of the transaction, she also ended up coordinating with the builder on many of the construction details that I probably should have handled, as the original purchaser.

When the completion date of the townhouse was delayed...and delayed...and delayed again, she kept everyone calm and committed to the deal. Even being the control freak that I am, at no time did I feel the need to intervene and take over—in fact, the reason I let Joan handle so many details that were probably my responsibility was because she was doing a better job than I would have! Ouch!

And, for the privilege of doing both her job and mine, she cheerfully paid me a 25% referral fee for my business.

A Great Buyer Agent...

Millie helped me buy three houses in Alabama. Even though Millie is one of the top agents in her city, I had her full attention during my first visit to the area.

I told Millie that I "must have" four bedrooms, a two-car garage and high-speed Internet. She showed me 15 homes in one day. One of them was priced $100,000 higher than the rest, but Millie thought it was an excellent investment and knew that I, as a real estate agent, would probably be interested. She was right. It was a great investment and met all my needs for a personal home in the interim. It needed just the right amount of work and was a perfect "paint and carpet" fix-n-flip. After our long day, it was my number one choice.

I told Millie I was ready to make an offer on the house. I figured she'd be excited about writing up my offer since the home was the most expensive one we'd looked at. Ka-ching for her! But she seemed reluctant to sell it to me. Nonetheless, I insisted and we made an appointment to write the offer on her listing the next day.

A few hours after we parted ways for the day, Millie called me to tell me about a listing she hadn't shown me because it only had three bedrooms. But after spending the day with me, she felt that it might just be The One. And she was right. The minute I drove onto the four-acre property in the woods, I was hooked. I don't think I've ever responded so emotionally to a home before. Where was the garage? No garage. High-speed Internet? Nope. Dial-up only. But Millie had seen how I had responded to other homes-in-the-country earlier and realized that a home-in-the-country was what I really wanted. So she found it for me even though I'd told her I was satisfied with and ready to buy the more expensive home in town. She even offered to pay me a referral fee; I didn't even ask. Cool.

A Great Buyer Agent for the Out of Town Investor (Me)

A few years ago, I attempted to buy an investment home in the Wilmington, North Carolina area. Nicole Lincoln, who was at Prudential Carolina at the time, was my real estate agent. I found her on the web—in fact, she was the only agent out of the five I e-mailed who responded to me. And I'm so glad she did. Nicole made me feel like her top priority during my visit and was always willing and able to switch gears when I found something new I wanted to explore.

I made an offer on a home three blocks from the ocean. She didn't bat an eye when I wanted to make a lowball offer or when I insisted on including all kinds of additional provisions in the contract that I felt were lacking in the standard North Carolina document. All in all, my offer was rather obnoxious. But she supported me 100% and never made me feel as if I was doing anything remotely inappropriate.

After some back and forth negotiation, I put the home under contract and returned home to Denver. Unfortunately, the home failed the inspection miserably and I terminated the contract under my inspection rights. Again, Nicole supported me 100% and never implied with word or tone that she was disappointed that I'd "wasted" so much of her time. If she was at all annoyed with me, she never let it show. That's class.

So...thanks Joan, Millie and Nicole! (If you'd like to contact any of my favorite real estate agents, just send me an e-mail at Jennifer@sellwithsoul.com and I'll hook you up.)

YOUR GUARDIAN ANGEL

I once listed a 1930's Tudor home for a friend of mine. It was adorable, showed reasonably well, lots of square footage for the money. My friend, the seller, told me that the sewer line had been replaced before she purchased the home, and I took her at her word. That's what she was told, and I didn't ask for any evidence. So, we advertised the home with a newer sewer line. The home didn't sell. And didn't sell. And didn't sell some more. My seller ran out of time, patience and money, so she terminated the listing and rented out the house.

One week after her renter moved in, my seller received a frantic phone call from the tenant that the sewer was backing up in the basement and had flooded everything. Turns out that the sewer line had never been replaced; it was the original clay line and was broken in several places. Either my seller was lied to when she purchased the home or she misunderstood a conversation; either way, she now had a very expensive and disruptive problem on her hands. Not to mention an angry tenant whose belongings had been damaged and was without sewer service for several days!

The moral of the story is twofold. First, when listing a property, always get evidence of repairs made, especially for items like sewer lines that are not visible to a buyer or his inspector. When you are working as a buyer agent, always request documentation of any high-ticket repairs made, so that your client is not blindsided the way my seller was when they go to sell.

But the real reason I tell you this story is this...throughout my real estate career, I have always felt a divine protection over my business. Other agents I have spoken with feel it too. Call it what you will—God, a guardian angel, whatever, but hopefully you will be blessed with one too.

The guardian angel protects you in your first year by allowing challenges no tougher than you can handle. Sure, you'll have some painful moments and you'll open your checkbook more than once, but you will be able to resolve most of the issues that arise, even as a beginner. As you become more knowledgeable and creative throughout your career, you will no doubt notice that the degree of difficulty of the real estate problems you encounter seems to increase with your growing competency!

My guardian angel continues to protect me in ways that sure don't seem like "protection." Specifically in not letting perfectly good listings sell. Let me explain.

Many times during my career, I have confidently listed a property at a good price and then watched it languish on the market for no apparent reason. Other similar homes are selling all around my listing, my seller is getting frustrated and both of us are mystified. We bury a St. Christopher statue in the yard, put three pennies under the welcome mat (a Feng Shui trick), and, of course, try price reductions, open houses, newspaper ads, etc. All to no avail. No offers, no real interest.

In the above example with the broken sewer line, let's pretend that the home did sell, and to make it more fun—let's assume the buyer was an attorney. Or married to one.

When that sewer line backed up into the basement after closing, who do you think would have gotten that first frantic phone call? My seller? Nope, me. Guess whose fault this whole mess would have been? My seller's? No again, mine. As a seller's agent, I advertised the home with a new sewer line and could easily have been held liable to make good on my advertising. In other words, I might have had to pay to have the sewer line replaced, as well as cover damage to the new owner's belongings. Sure, my seller would have some liability too, but I'm sure you can see how this situation would be ugly for me.

So, I believe my guardian angel protected me by not allowing the home to sell. As frustrating as it was for all of us, it was a good lesson. One I have learned again and again. In nearly all situations where a good listing isn't selling, we later discover the reason why...either the seller's situation changed and the sale of the home would have been disastrous for them personally, or there were latent defects that appeared after the listing was withdrawn, or there was some problem in the home that had to be fixed before it would be "allowed" to sell.

I once marketed and eventually sold a house that had been rebuilt after a significant fire. The home was a 1950's ranch-style home in a marginal neighborhood. Because the insurance company completely restored the home after the fire, it was the most updated home available in the neighborhood. Brand new kitchen, new baths, new windows, new roof, new systems, new plumbing. Most homes in the neighborhood had not been updated and showed poorly. My seller was willing to price the home competitively and I expected it to fly off the market with multiple offers.

It did not. In fact, we went two months without a single showing. In an active market. I was stunned. No amount of advertising seemed to generate any additional interest. We lowered the price several times with no effect. The home was now thousands under market value and still no interest.

One day I stopped by the house for my weekly Fluff & Flush visit and noticed a strong smoke smell permeating the home that hadn't been there before. I thought it was odd, but, to be honest with you, hoped it was my imagination and that it would go away. I went back to the house the following week and the smell was worse. I notified my sellers (who lived out of state) of the problem and they authorized me to hire a company who specialized in removing odors from homes. After three attempts to remove the smell, the odor-eliminator company admitted defeat.

To cut to the chase, it turned out that one burned stud in a bedroom wall had not been replaced in the restoration of the home, and in the heat of the summer, the charred wood started to smell. The contractor who did the work replaced the stud and the smell went away entirely. Within four days, we had seven showings and a full price offer.

I knew it was my guardian angel protecting me from selling the home. Until we solved the problem, that home was going to sit there. Now, whenever I have a listing that is inexplicably not selling, I describe the guardian angel phenomenon to my seller and ask him to open his mind to potential issues that might be holding back the sale of his home.

Ya Do What Ya Gotta Do...

There are times in real estate (lots of 'em) when you will go above and beyond the call of duty (in your humble opinion) in order to please your client, secure your paycheck or simply because it's the right thing to do. As you gain experience, these "opportunities" will appear to lessen, but perhaps only because you now realize they are part of your job, or you've gotten better at delegating such duties back to your client...who probably should have taken care of them in the first place.

For example, what if you show up to do an open house, fresh cookies and sign-in sheets in hand...and the beds are unmade? You probably won't discover this until your seller has left, or if you do notice it, you might not have the guts to say anything—after all, if the seller doesn't care, why should you? But hopefully you do care, so go make the beds. Sure, I know you'd really rather not, but do it anyway.

Or what about that $800,000 spec home listing you have with the dusty contractor footprints across the "gleaming" Brazilian cherry floors? I can't tell you how many times I've mopped the floors of my listings to make sure they show their best.

How about the lawn of a vacant listing that is dying due to lack of water? Yes, I have spent all afternoon watering my client's yard. Just sat in the house with my cell phone and a good book, moving the sprinkler around every 20 minutes or so. I once had a cleaning "party" with the listing agent of a condo my buyers were closing on later that day. Three hours prior to the closing, we could be found in rubber gloves scrubbing toilets, dusting ceiling fans, cleaning baseboards.

Yeah, real estate is so glamorous. Once I waited in the alley at 7:00 a.m. for the garbage truck. My buyer client was under contract to purchase an older home (1920's vintage) with a one-car detached garage that was entered from the alley (typical in old Denver). However, a Denver city dumpster sat directly across the alley from the garage door, which made entry into the garage impossible. There wasn't enough room to make the turn.

I called the Denver Waste Management Department and asked them to move the dumpster so my client could access his garage. They told me the only way to ensure the relocation of the dumpster was to catch the trash men on trash day. So there I was, standing in an alley, morning coffee in hand, waiting for the garbage truck to come through.

Once I painted the interior of a house for my client. Would I do that again? Uh, no. It was a ridiculous thing for me to do—my clients were not destitute, far from it, and they certainly could have hired a professional painter. But I was enthusiastic and, for some crazy reason, it seemed like a good idea at the time. My enthusiasm must have been contagious because I even got my assistant to help me!

Anyway, this good deed ended up being worth doing. When my sellers told their friends, Darren and Samantha, about my painting "service," they were so impressed they hired me to sell their $400,000 home and be the buyer agent on their replacement $600,000 home! So, in reality, I was paid over $20,000 for my painting efforts. I can't promise this will happen to you every time, but you never know.

IF IT FEELS WRONG, DON'T DO IT

Sometimes you'll be presented with a deal that feels good, but just doesn't feel right. Maybe you feel that you're taking advantage of a situation or that you're getting a paycheck you really don't deserve. Other agents tell you to take the money and run—after all, there are plenty of times you work hard and don't get paid for it. But that little voice inside you is telling you different.

I worked with a client who wanted to buy a piece of property on which to build a custom home. To be clear, this was not a home in a new subdivision, it was just a buildable lot on the outskirts of town. The lot was around $100,000; the home he wanted to build would be around $500,000. I found him the lot and put it under contract. He went out and found a general contractor to build him his custom home. Apparently, it is common practice for the real estate agent to get paid a commission on the final price of the home, even though my involvement with the construction of the home was nil. Nada. I certainly wasn't going to negotiate the cost of lumber or otherwise involve myself in the building process. Even my buyer seemed okay with paying me on the final price, but it just felt wrong.

Following my conscience, I declined to assert my "right" to a commission on the construction of his home and just took a fee on the purchase of the lot. I wish I could say that my ethical behavior resulted in a flood of referrals from my buyer, but it didn't really. I feel good about it anyway. That's enough.

Another time I agreed to facilitate a sale between related parties. A woman bought her brother's house and asked me to put the paperwork together. We agreed on a fee of $1,000 for my real estate services. I prepared the contract, explained it to both parties, and delivered the contract to the lender and title company. All in all, it took me two hours, tops. Since it was a friendly transaction, there was no inspection to negotiate and no other problems arose. The loan went through smoothly and as it turned out, I couldn't even attend the closing because I was out of town. I felt guilty accepting the $1,000 fee for two hours work, so I returned it. I just didn't feel right charging $500/hour for something that was so easy for me to do.

Show some respect and empathy for your clients. At the least, try not to embarrass yourself and the industry by gouging people whenever the opportunity presents itself. Maybe they won't complain to your face, but believe me, they notice. People aren't stupid and they aren't gullible. You might get their money, but it's never worth it if the real cost is your self-respect, or if you don't care about that, your reputation in the community.

Don't get me wrong, you do work for free a lot and deserve nice paychecks for your efforts. But that isn't a blank check to overcharge people unfairly. They may not even openly balk at your fee, but it wouldn't hurt to "take advantage" of the opportunity to do a good deed and improve the reputation of the real estate community!

To Wrap Up
A Few Words of Encouragement

Do you ever look at the Sunday real estate section of the newspaper and see all those smiling faces looking out at you? All that competition? I did when I was new and it was quite intimidating. So many real estate agents, all with more experience and expertise than I had—how was I ever going to break into the business? Surely all my friends already knew five or six agents who had been serving their family for generations...

Surprise, they probably don't! The vast majority of your friends and acquaintances have no real loyalty to any real estate agent. They'll be happy to work with you if you approach them right. And, if you're new, this is one place the public's lack of appreciation for the real estate industry can work for you!

Since real estate looks so easy, many times your inexperience won't be a factor if your friends consider you a reasonably competent human being. They think real estate agents just hold open houses and drive buyers around and, in the beginning, let 'em think that. They may not be too concerned about finding someone more experienced...after all, how hard can it be? Of course, when you have a few years under your belt, you will certainly use your experience to your advantage when competing against a freshman agent who is a friend of the family, but as a rookie, don't fret about it too much.

There is plenty of business out there, there really is. If you can sell 20 homes a year, you should be able to pay the bills. That's only 20 people out of your whole town who have to hire you. Just because you're new doesn't mean that you have to start at the bottom. You are not lined up behind all those smiling faces in the Sunday paper. You can jump right in and see them next year at the Board of Realtors® annual awards luncheon.

Question Convention

As you go through your real estate career, you will get a lot of advice from your broker, other agents, teachers and trainers. If something doesn't sound right to you, don't assume it is. Real estate is full of interesting (and some not-so) characters who don't deserve the benefit of the doubt just because they have more experience than you do. I ignored almost all of the advice I got through the years. Real estate has a lot of gray areas and you can almost always find multiple solutions to the problems you face. Don't be afraid to go with your gut instinct. If you're selling with soul, I can guarantee that you won't regret it.

RANDOM REFLECTIONS

So, what do I mean by "An Extraordinary Career?" Ah, I'm glad you asked me that. But first, let me ask you...what do you think I mean? Or, in other words, what would make a career "extraordinary" for you?

Clearly, "extraordinary" means different things to different people. To some, it means making gobs and gobs of money, and that's nothing to be ashamed of. And, by the way, entirely possible in real estate. To others, it means having a career that makes you want to jump out of bed in the morning and get started (and making gobs and gobs of money). Some would consider their career extraordinary if it helped them help others. How about building a business to pass on to your children? Or a career that allows you the flexibility to travel or spend more time with family? Or to retire early?

A career in real estate offers all of these benefits and more. After twelve years in the business, here's what my life looks like—I divide my time equally between selling real estate and writing about selling real estate, and am able to make a very comfortable living without ever working more than 30 hours a week. As a result of my strong sphere of influence, I never prospect; my phone rings, I answer it, and I have a new client. I go to Mexico or the Caribbean at least three times a year; I could go more often, but I've always loved my job and haven't needed to "get away" from it. I took a sabbatical of sorts five years ago and was able to live comfortably on my savings for six months before I got bored enough to go back to work. I typically own six rental properties at a time and I buy and sell at least three every year, which keeps the dogs fed and gives me a nice petty cash fund.

I've never dreaded mornings or Mondays; in fact during the peak of my career, I never took more than a four-day vacation because I truly loved my job...I couldn't stand to be away that long! I am proud of the business I created and while I won't claim that everybody loves me (I got over that fantasy early on), I do believe that I made more people happy than unhappy. And, I helped several of my clients make their own gobs and gobs of money with their real estate investments.

How does all this sound to you? If you're new, you probably won't be enjoying such a lifestyle this year or next, but it can happen quicker than you think. And in the meantime, if you're selling with your soul, you will enjoy working hard, you will be proud of the business you build and yes, you will make a comfortable living, perhaps even an extraordinary one.

Your career will be extraordinary if you follow your heart, do what feels natural and work damn hard. Okay, so working damn hard might not feel natural, but you might be surprised how hard you're happy to work when you're thrilled with and proud of what you're doing.

So...best wishes on your real estate career. I hope I've been helpful. Contrary to popular belief (and my own fantasies) most authors do not lead a glamorous life of chatting with Oprah and attending book release bashes. Well, hell, maybe they do, but I don't. Anyway, my point is that I can probably help you out if you want more information on any ideas or suggestions you found in this book. Or, if you want someone to bounce your own outside-the-box ideas off of...drop me a line!

Go get 'em.

appendix

CHECKLISTS
- Buyer-Under-Contract Checklist
- New Listing Checklist
- Listing-Under-Contract Checklist
- HOA Questionnaire for the Listing Agent
- Information Sheet for Condominium Buyers

RESOURCES
- Law of Attraction
- Recommended Books
- Online Real Estate Forums
- Vendors

CONTRIBUTORS (IN ALPHABETICAL ORDER)
- Jim Bonner
- Janie Coffey
- Sarah Cooper
- Kenneth W. Edwards
- Ashley Drake Gephart
- Susan Haughton
- John MacArthur
- Gary Miljour
- Bryant Tutas

BUYER-UNDER-CONTRACT CHECKLIST

This checklist can be used in paper form, or input into your contact management system. It was created specifically to be used with Top Producer, but will probably work with most systems. Refer to Chapter Eight for more details on each item. As contract-to-closing protocol varies significantly by market area, be sure to confirm the accuracy and appropriateness of each item in your jurisdiction.

activity	due date
Enter contract dates into contact management program	Day of Contract
Fax contract to lender	Day of Contract
Deliver property disclosures to buyer	Day of Contract
Deliver earnest money to listing agent	Day of Contract
Give buyer HOA contact information & questionnaire	Day of Contract
Give buyer inspector names & numbers	Day of Contract
Call buyer's lender to confirm loan application	1st Week after Contract
Call buyer's lender to discuss scheduling appraisal	1st Week after Contract
Deliver signed disclosures to listing agent	1st Week after Contract
Tell buyer to look into homeowner hazard insurance	1st Week after Contract
Call buyer's lender to check in	1st Week after Contract
Has closing been scheduled?	1st Week after Contract
Is buyer doing a mail-out close or POA?	2nd Week after Contract
Are the inspection items done?	1 Week before Closing
Get documentation of inspection repairs	1 Week before Closing
Schedule walk-thru	1 Week before Closing

activity	due date
Remind buyer to transfer utilities	1 Week before Closing
Send any changes to lender and/or title company	2-4 Days before Closing
Confirm closing time & place	2-4 Days before Closing
Review closing figures with buyer	2-4 Days before Closing
Tell buyer to bring driver's license & cashier's check to closing	2-4 Days before Closing
Prepare the file for closing	Right before Closing
Turn the file in to the office manager	Right after Closing
Add buyer to your SOI (or change buyer's address)	Right after Closing
Add buyer to your post-closing follow-up program	Right after Closing
Call buyer to check on move	4 Days after Closing

A printable version of this checklist is available at www.SellwithSoul.com

New Listing Checklist for Listing Agents

This checklist can be used in paper form, or input into your contact management system. It was created specifically to be used with Top Producer, but will probably work with most systems. Refer to Chapter Ten for more details on each specific item.

activity	due date
Seller signature on all listing contracts & disclosures	Prior to MLS entry
Take pictures	Prior to MLS entry
Schedule/create the Virtual Tour	Day of MLS entry
Get the key, install the lockbox	Day of MLS entry
Get HOA contact information from seller	Day of MLS entry
Enter the listing on MLS	Day of MLS entry
Enter the listing on your contact manager program	Day of MLS entry
Order 'Just Listed' cards	Day of MLS entry
Track the expiration date	Day of MLS entry
Install the For Sale sign	Day of MLS entry
Showing information to showing desk/showing service	Day of MLS entry
Create & display 'Special Features' cards in the home	Day of MLS entry
Send a copy of the MLS listing to the seller	Day of MLS entry
Deliver copies of all signed documents to seller	1 Day after MLS entry
Prepare the home brochure	1 Day after MLS entry
Schedule open house/put up Open Sunday sign rider	1 Day after MLS entry
Call the HOA to verify information (See checklist)	1st week after MLS entry
Deliver home brochures to home	When ready
Solicit feedback, provide to seller	1st week after MLS entry
Load Internet advertising	1st week after MLS entry

activity	due date
Email web links to seller	1st week after MLS entry
Fluff & Flush 1	7 Days after MLS entry
First market report to seller	7 Days after MLS entry
Call Seller "Are the showing instructions working for you?"	7 Days after MLS entry
Preview new competing listings/report findings to seller	2nd week after MLS entry
Fluff & Flush 2	2nd week after MLS entry
Call seller "Need more brochures yet?"	2nd week after MLS entry
Fluff & Flush 3 (continue every week)	3rd week after MLS entry
Call seller to check in	3rd week after MLS entry
Second market report to seller	3rd week after MLS entry
Preview new competing listings/report findings to seller	4th week after MLS entry
Prepare & schedule 6 week CMA meeting/3rd market update	6th week after MLS entry
Pick up brochure box	6th week after MLS entry
Re-do exterior photos?	When season changes
Fourth market update to seller	8th week after MLS entry

A printable version of this checklist is available at www.SellwithSoul.com

LISTING-UNDER-CONTRACT CHECKLIST

This checklist can be used in paper form, or input into your contact management system. It was created specifically to be used with Top Producer, but will probably work with most systems. Refer to Chapter Ten for more details on each item. As contract-to-closing protocol varies significantly by market area, be sure to confirm the accuracy and appropriateness of each item in your specific jurisdiction.

activity	due date
Get the earnest money check	Day of Contract
Turn in contract file to office manager	Day of Contract
Enter contract dates into your contract manager program	Day of Contract
Order title work and HOA documents	Day of Contract
Change the status in the MLS	Day of Contract
Notify showing desk/showing service of status change	Day of Contract
Notify agents with showing appointments of status change	Day of Contract
Send property disclosures to the buyer agent	Day of Contract
Call buyer's lender and introduce yourself	1st Week after Contract
Pick up the brochure box	1st Week after Contract
Get payoff information from seller	1st Week after Contract
Property disclosures returned from buyer with signature?	1st Week after Contract
Put up SOLD sign	2nd Week after Contract
Call buyer's lender	2nd Week after Contract
Prepare for the appraisal	2nd Week after Contract
Set the closing	2nd Week after Contract
Confirm that the inspection items are complete	1 Week before Closing
Confirm that seller has arranged cleaning	1 Week before Closing
Arrange mail-out close or POA	1 Week before Closing
Send any changes to lender and/or title company	1 Week before Closing

activity	due date
Is the buyer doing a walk-thru?	1 Week before Closing
Confirm closing time, date & place with all parties	1 Week before Closing
Review closing figures	1-2 Days before Closing
Remind seller to bring driver's license to closing	1-2 Days before Closing
Order earnest money check from office manager	1-2 Days before Closing
Prepare the file for closing	1-2 Days before Closing
Pick up the sign, lockbox and interior brochure box	Day of Closing
Turn in closed file to office manager	Right after Closing
Notify showing desk/showing service of closed	Right after Closing
Add seller to post-closing follow -up plan	1-2 Days after Closing
Update seller's address in your SOI	1-2 Days after Closing
Call seller after move-out	3-5 Days after Closing
Update websites with sale	3-5 Days after Closing

A printable version of this checklist is available at www.SellwithSoul.com

HOA QUESTIONNAIRE FOR THE LISTING AGENT

As discussed in Chapters Ten and Twelve, this form is to be used when you've listed a property that has a homeowner's association (HOA). Right after you've executed the listing agreement, call the HOA to gather and/or confirm the information below. This will help you market the property correctly and avoid surprises during the contract-to-closing period.

Spoke with:_____

Date: _____

Are there any restrictions on For Sale/Open House Signs?: _____

What is the monthly management fee?: _____

What does it cover? Heat, Water/Sewer, Insurance,
Roof, Pool/Tennis, Snow Removal, Trash, Other? _____

_____

_____

_____

_____

_____

_____

_____

Do you expect the fee to increase in the near future?: _____

What is the transfer fee at sale?: _____

How much is the working capital/reserve deposit?: _____

Is the working capital/reserve refundable at sale?: _____

Are there any special assessments coming up?: _____

Is the building/project FHA-approved?: _____

Whom should an interested buyer contact if they have questions?

    Name:_____

    Phone Number: _____

Whom do I contact for financials, minutes, etc?

    Name:_____

    Phone Number: _____

Any other information, e.g., pet restrictions, upcoming improvements, etc.?

_____
_____
_____
_____
_____
_____
_____

A printable version of this checklist is available at www.SellwithSoul.com

Information Sheet for Condominium Buyers

As discussed in Chapters Eight and Twelve, this form is to be given to buyers who are considering purchasing a property that has a homeowners association (HOA). You should instruct the buyer to contact the HOA him or herself and ask the questions below.

When you purchase a condominium or townhome, you will automatically belong to the Homeowners Association (HOA). Every HOA is a little different, with individual strengths and weaknesses. It is in your best interest to contact the HOA to judge for yourself if you are comfortable with the fees, the rules and regulations, the financial stability of the association and the way the HOA is managed and organized.

Please call: _____,

prior to: _____,

and ask the following questions:

What is the monthly management fee and what does it cover?: _____

Are there any planned or contemplated special assessments coming up?: ____

Do you have a "working capital" deposit required of new homeowners?: ____
How much is it? Is it refundable on sale?: _____

Do you have any restrictions (e.g., pets, children, smoking)that I should be aware of?: _____

Are you planning to make any improvementsto the property in the near future?: _____

Are there any special move-in procedures or costs I need to know about?

_____

_____

_____

Is there anything else a potential buyer of the property should know?

_____

_____

Depending on the property, you may also want to ask about the age of the heating system and roof, guest parking, barbecue grill restrictions, etc.

I acknowledge that I have been given this Condominium Buyer Information Sheet by _____

of _____,

and agree to contact the Home Owners Association with any questions or concerns I may have about the HOA and/or the project itself.

Buyer: _____

Date: _____

Buyer: _____

Date: _____

A printable version of this checklist is available at www.SellwithSoul.com

RESOURCES

Law of Attraction

The Success Principles, by Jack Canfield – www.thesuccessprinciples.com

The Secret – www.thesecret.tv

Recommended books

The Success Principles, by Jack Canfield

20 Day to the Top! by Brian Sullivan

Your Successful Real Estate Career, by Dr. Kenneth Edwards

The Complete Idiot's Guide to Success as a Real Estate Agent,
by Marilyn Sullivan

Paying the Price, by Madge Wells

The Consultative Real Estate Agent, by Kelle Sparta

Don't Sweat the Small Stuff about Money, by Richard Carlson, Ph.D.

The Introvert Advantage, by Marti Olsen Laney

High Probability Selling, by Jacques Werth and Nicholas E. Ruben

Online Real Estate Forums

Active Rain – www.activerain.com

Agents Online – www.agentsonline.net

Wanna Network – www.wannanetwork.com

Vendors

Efax – receive your faxes online – www.efax.com

Constant Contact – easily create online newsletters
www.constantcontact.com

Top Producer – manage your contact database and much more
www.topproducer.com

Gary Hall – an excellent resource for contact management systems www.
garydavidhall.com

Real Estate Shows – do-it-yourself virtual tours
www.realestateshows.com

CPG Tours – another do-it-yourself virtual tour company
www.cpgtours.com

The CE Shop – online continuing education
www.theCEshop.com

Expired Plus – a soulful program for prospecting Expireds
www.expiredplus.com

CONTRIBUTORS

THANKS Janie, JMac, Ashley, Broker Bryant, Jim, Sarah, Susan, DocKen and Gary for your contributions to Sell with Soul... and for your friendship, of course.

Jim Bonner
In my 10-year real estate sales career, I can honestly say that I've never had a long-term relationship with a lender. Eventually, they all seemed to disappoint me, and there's always another one right around the corner. Jim is the exception. I met him early in my career, was delighted by his service and continue to be so. Jim's calm disposition soothes first-time buyers like you wouldn't believe and he really knows his stuff. Jim owns his own mortgage company—J. Allston Mortgage. Drop by and say HI and tell him Jennifer sent you! www.JAllston.com.

Janie Coffey
When I decided I wanted to live in South Florida, I contacted Janie from her Active Rain blog. I could tell she had tons of personality, a lot of smarts, and a wealth of area knowledge. I had every confidence that she would take great care of me. And she did. I didn't end up moving to South Florida, but if I ever do, you can bet that Janie is my go-to gal. Check her out at www.activerain. com/janiec or her own company's website at www.PapillonRealEstate.com

Sarah Cooper
I also met Sarah on Active Rain and you should too. Sarah is one of the site's most popular contributors and once you've read her stuff, you'll know why. And, you'll feel that you know HER. Sarah sells real estate in Hurricane, West Virginia and I know she's loved by all who are blessed to know her. When you have time to bury yourself in her writings, check out www.theputnamscoop. com. You'll soon be hooked!
You can contact Sarah at wv.agent@yahoo.com.

Kenneth W. Edwards
If you enjoyed Sell with Soul, you'll love Ken's book *Your Successful Real Estate Career*. While Ken and I approach a real estate sales career from a similar perspective, you'll find that his book covers topics I left out, and vice versa. He's funny, smart, irreverent and an all-around great guy.
Check him out—you'll be glad you did.
You can reach Doctor Ken at DoctorKenisin@aol.com.

Ashley Drake Gephart

Ashley is another cyber friend of mine—I think I met her through Agents Online, but I can't remember. She's been a fantastic resource for me and is definitely your soulful connection in the Albuquerque area. Ashley is organized, intelligent, caring and a fascinating person! Check out her website at www. ExpertRealEstateTalk.com or email her at Ashley@AshleySellsHouses.com.

Susan Haughton

Susan is my long-lost soul sister. We're so alike it's scary. Susan has terrific perspectives on the nuances of selling real estate respectfully and her track record proves that she's onto something. She's a master "SOI-er" and, like me, has never cold-called or knocked on a stranger's door for business. I have a special file on my computer for Susan's wisdom that I collect through her participation on the same online forums I hang out on. Susan "gets" it. If you ever need an agent in the Alexandria, Virginia area, Susan is your gal. I guarantee you'll be delighted. www.susanmovesyou.com.

John MacArthur

Ah, JMac, my newfound friend and biggest fan. First and foremost an artist, passionately dedicated to rebuilding New Orleans, John is a fascinating fellow. He's interesting and wickedly intelligent and if he has an opinion on something—it's worth reading. Twice. Like Susan, he "gets" it and I'd be crazy not to hire him to be my real estate agent if I'm ever shopping in the Bethesda, Maryland area. Check him out at www.themacarthurgroup.com or send an email to macarthurgroup@gmail.com.

Gary Miljour

Gary is a mortgage broker in Tempe Arizona and a darn fine one at that. If you enjoy fluff, propaganda or subject-dodging, Gary is definitely NOT your man. He'll tell it like it is...and then get it done for you. Learn more about Gary at www.garymiljour.com or www.activerain.com/blogs/gmiljour

Bryant Tutas

Broker Bryant Tutas—what can I say? BB is among the elite contributors to Active Rain, and, like Sarah Cooper, is absolutely addictive to read. He KNOWs how to sell real estate, even his nearly impossible market of Poinciana, Florida. Professional, fun, knowledgeable and utterly soulful, BB is what we all should strive to be in our real estate careers. Watch for his book coming soon! www.brokerbryant.com.

If you enjoyed *Sell with Soul,* you'll love
*If You're Not Having Fun Selling Real Estate, You're Not Doing
it Right: Mastering the Art of Selling with Soul*

Available at the Sell with Soul Bookstore
www.SWSStore.com
or
www.Amazon.com

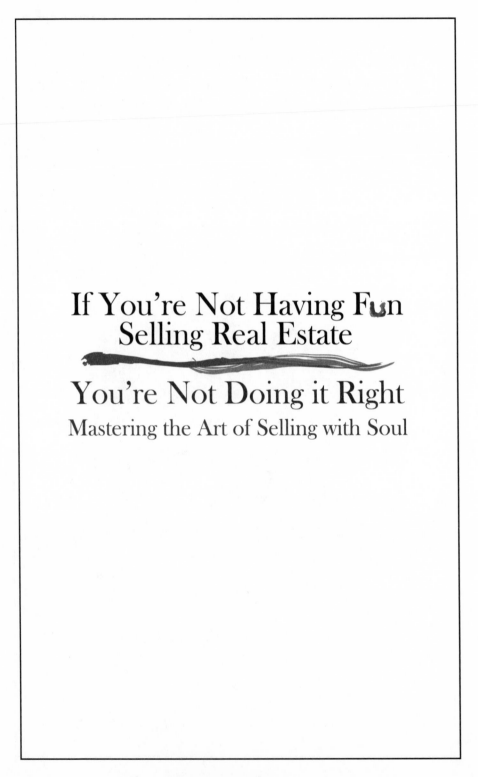

If You're Not Having Fun
Selling Real Estate

You're Not Doing it Right
Mastering the Art of Selling with Soul

Chapter Three

Prospecting with Soul

All rightee... let's get the ball rolling with a topic near and dear to every real estate agent's heart. Generating business. Good business. Loyal business. Consistent business. And, if you're anything like me, you'd prefer to generate this good, loyal and consistent business using methods that don't force you too far out of your comfort zone or make you feel... well... icky. Methods that don't make you dread getting up in the morning!

The official term for generating business is "prospecting." I found several different definitions of the word, but one of the most succinct was: "The process of identifying and qualifying potential customers." Sounds harmless enough, doesn't it? So why does the word "prospecting" get such a bad rap among all but the most outgoing, aggressive salespeople?

Well, I can't speak for the rest of the world, but for me, the term "prospecting" has become synonymous with "pestering." When I'm prospected to, I'm usually annoyed by it. Or, at the very least, indifferent. I hang up on telemarketers; I throw away junk mail; I hide when the doorbell rings. When I'm taken to lunch or out for coffee by a mortgage broker, title representative or insurance agent, I'm in full armor waiting for the inevitable sales pitch (and I confess that I'm often tempted to cancel in anticipation of it).

As real estate agents, we're trained to prospect religiously! Every day! To make room on our calendars for our daily prospecting and not let anything interfere with it! If we don't prospect on a regular basis, our businesses are doomed to failure! And it's our own fault for allowing anything (even our pesky clients) to distract us from our sole purpose in life—to find new targets for our well-rehearsed sales pitches!

Blech.

I got into this business because I thought I might enjoy selling houses. I didn't know much about the actual process of selling houses, but from what I'd seen, it looked like fun. Frankly, it had never occurred to me that I would be responsible for finding people to sell houses to; like many new agents, I just figured I'd get my real estate license and, well, start selling houses!

So, it came as a surprise to me when my first broker informed me that I was responsible for drumming up business for myself. That wasn't anything I'd given much thought to. What was an even bigger surprise was when my broker told me that not only was I responsible for finding my own business, but that the best way to do that was to call up strangers on the phone and knock on my neighbors' doors asking for business. Oh, and spend a bunch of money mailing postcards and newsletters to my chosen "farm" area.

This didn't sound like much fun to me. But not only did it not sound like fun, it didn't sound like something that would actually work. I can't remember the last time I bought anything from a cold-caller or hurried to the phone to respond to a mailed marketing piece. So, why would I promote myself to other people using techniques that don't work on me? It seemed kind of silly.

This was back in 1996, before I could even spell "Google." If it sounded kind of silly then, it's outrageously ridiculous today.

I'm quickly reaching the conclusion that an awful lot of traditional marketing doesn't work. Even if it used to work, it doesn't anymore. Oh, sure, people are being paid very well to create marketing products and strategies and systems, but are these products and strategies and systems actually reaching the end consumer?

I don't fancy myself any sort of economic analyst, so I won't pretend to have done much research into the matter; I can only speak for myself and for the people I know with whom I've had this conversation. Our consensus is that, no, the vast majority of marketing that crosses our radar on a daily basis does not persuade us to make a purchase we wouldn't otherwise be tempted to make. I suppose the argument can be made that we don't realize the impact marketing has on our brand awareness, and I'll buy that. I'm sure there's a not-so-good reason I prefer one brand over another that has something to do with a marketing effort, but that's not what we're talking about here.

We're talking about YOU. YOU, the small business owner/real estate agent who doesn't have even a fraction of the budget necessary to implement a pow-erful-enough marketing campaign to create a nationally recognizable brand. Or probably even a city-wide recognizable brand.

Here's the thing. No one particularly likes being marketed to. We open our mail over the trash can; we put No Solicitors signs on our doors; we hang up on telemarketers and we take a bathroom break during commercials (if we haven't already TIVO'ed out those pesky advertisements). I get loads of junk mail in my real estate office mailbox, and I no longer bother to go through it- it gets sent straight to the recycle bin. When a loan officer or title representa-tive knocks on my office door asking if I'll give him a chance to "earn my busi-ness," I smile politely, send him on his way and promptly forget about him. I get dozens of emails every day from people I'm vaguely familiar with, asking me to try their new products (for free!)—and I delete them, even though I'm sure many of the products are actually worth looking at.

Heck, the other day, I was looking through my local neighborhood newspaper for an ad I thought I'd seen for a new hair salon and I had to actually force myself to see the advertising instead of automatically skipping over it looking for a news item of interest. I found it incredibly difficult to acknowledge the ads because I've trained myself to ignore them.

You're probably the same way, am I right?

When I want information about something, I go to the Internet. I don't need a salesperson at my door, on my computer screen or in my mailbox to provide information on their product. I can look it up myself, thank you very much, and get the details I need, including non-partisan opinions of said product!

Stop Wasting Your Time (and Money) Marketing to Me!

I recently initiated an online discussion between mortgage brokers and real estate agents as to the best way for a mortgage broker to attract business from agents. Basically, I advised mortgage brokers that all their fancy marketing was utterly wasted on us real estate agent-types and that all we want from our go-to-mortgage guy or gal was exceptional service when they're working on one of our deals. Get me to the closing table, make me look good to my client, and you're golden. Especially in today's crazy mortgage environment, there's no way some fluffy marketing piece is going to convince me to entrust my precious buyer deals to someone I've not worked with before.

The mortgage community seemed startled by my assertion that their marketing was a waste of time and money. I found this interesting on many levels. First, something that utterly perplexes me about those involved in the real estate industry is our apparent inability to consider the effect of our marketing techniques on the marketee—that is—the person we're assaulting with our sales pitch. Those who detest telemarketers and were first in line to sign up for the Do Not Call list rabidly defend their own cold-calling campaigns. And those who complain about the mountain of advertising that appears in their office mailbox often generate plenty of their own and fill others' inboxes with it. But that's a soapbox for a different chapter.

Second, it just seems so obvious, especially in today's mortgage market, that performance will far outweigh prospecting as an effective self-promotion technique. But I guess it's not (obvious). One of the mortgage brokers who participated in the conversation made the statement—"Well, shouldn't you give us a chance before you just dismiss us as incompetent?" Uh, no. Not saying that you are incompetent, but I'll admit to a level of Guilty Until Proven Innocent when it comes to my mortgage business. The ability to put together (or pay someone to put together) a pretty brochure just isn't going to convince me of your getting-the-deal-to-closing abilities. Not even a little tiny bit. In fact, I might worry that you're spending all your time marketing and not enough time getting-your-deals-to-closing!

Okay, so if we agree that marketing doesn't work the magic it used to... or any at all... then what? WHAT can you do to bring business your way? (Stay tuned—we'll get to that shortly)

Promise me...

Before I continue, let me make a little disclaimer here. There are many paths to success in a real estate business, and I'm not so arrogant as to believe that mine is the only "right" path. In fact, I'll go so far as to proclaim that while MY way is perfect for me, YOUR way (not mine) will be perfect for you. And here's what I mean by YOUR way:

Commit to me that you will build your real estate business using techniques and strategies that feel right to you. That feel natural and comfortable. That strike you as... intelligent. Before you commit to a new prospecting approach, ask your gut how it feels about it. Are you excited to expose your world to this latest technique? Are you proud of it? Would it work on you? Or... are you mentally arguing with your gut, trying to convince it that you're doing the right thing, even though you're flooded with misgivings?

Trust those misgivings. If you're not proud of what you're getting ready to do, something is wrong. Maybe you just need to make a little tweak, or maybe you need to start all over from scratch. But it's worth the effort to discover YOUR way. And running a real estate business YOUR way is a lot of fun!

Traditional sales trainers will tell you to ignore your gut, buck up and Just Do It. Don't let your fear get in the way of your paycheck! Remember, real estate is a Numbers Game, so even if you're rejected over and over again, be assured that eventually you'll reach that one golden "yes" that will make all those people you irritated irrelevant! Thicken your skin or you'll never succeed!

Again, BLECH.

If I'm scared to do something, I figure there's a good reason I'm scared. And even if there isn't, unless I really, really, really want to overcome that fear, I'll look for alternatives so I can stay in my comfort zone. Why not? I like being comfortable!

So, with that said, I'll share with you how I built a successful real estate career without ever thickening my skin, venturing out of my comfort zone or pestering a soul. MY way.